The Songs of Wild Birds

Wood Thrush

The Songs of Wild Birds

Winter Wren

Lang Elliott

with photos and sound recordings
by the author and others

Houghton Mifflin Company
Boston   New York
2006

Rose-breasted Grosbeak

For information about permission to reproduce selections from this book, write to Permissions, Houghton Mifflin Company, 215 Park Avenue South, New York, New York 10003.

Visit our Web site: www.houghtonmifflinbooks.com.

Library of Congress Cataloging-in-Publication Data

Elliott, Lang.
   The songs of wild birds / Lang Elliott with photos and sound recordings by the author and others.
       p. cm.
   Includes bibliographical references and index.
   ISBN-13: 978-0-618-66398-9
   ISBN-10: 0-618-66398-3
   1. Birdsongs. 2. Songbirds. I. Title.
     QL698.5.E457 2006
     598.159'4—dc22   2006009766

Book design by Lang Elliott,
NatureSound Studio, P.O. Box 84,
Ithaca, New York 14851-0084

Excerpt from *Spring in Washington* by Louis J. Halle. Copyright 1947, 1957. Reprinted by permission of the Audubon Naturalist Society of the Central Atlantic States.

Excerpt from "The Oven Bird" from *The Poetry of Robert Frost* edited by Edward Connery Lathem. Copyright 1916, 1969 by Henry Holt and Company. Copyright 1944 by Robert Frost. Reprinted by permission of Henry Holt and Company, LLC.

Printed in China

C&C 10 9 8 7 6 5 4 3 2 1

Mourning Dove

Contents

Veery

Foreword

From the outset, they knew he was different. "They" were the typical Cornell undergrads — young, bright, competitive, and well focused on the science of bird song. He was a little older and noticeably wiser, more relaxed I sensed, and interested not only in good biology but also in some of the larger questions of aesthetics, philosophy, and the poetry of life itself. And he knew well many of the birds the students were only reading about. It was during that semester-long bird song seminar that I led at Cornell University in the fall of 1993 that I first got to know Lang Elliott.

We bicycled together that fall, too, riding the hilly terrain of the Ithaca countryside, taking in the autumn colors and listening to whatever birds would oblige. We marveled at the outbursts of flickers and Pileated Woodpeckers, at the fussing notes of chickadees and nuthatches, and took great pleasure in hearing snippets of bird song, as a few young birds practiced their melodies before the onset of winter.

Not long after, we talked at length about science and art, about their differences in approach, and Lang outlined his plans to bridge the gap between the two disciplines with his book and compact disc *Music of the Birds: A Celebration of Bird Song,* of which I was to be the content editor. Working with Lang was a pleasure. I increasingly valued the way Lang saw and heard the world, and he helped broaden my perspective on bird song and science.

Most recently, in the spring of 2005, we spent time in the field recording birds together, in coastal New Jersey. I found myself obsessed with a robin in the campground, partly because it was the only bird I found singing, but Lang walked down a path to a seeming paradise where he captured some of the richest sounds I have ever heard recorded.

In *The Songs of Wild Birds,* you're invited to come and listen with Lang, too. Walk down that path to the paradise that he inevitably finds in the field, slip your headphones on, and feast on the sights and sounds of our singing planet. Join Lang as bitterns sound off in a North Dakota marsh; as puffins snore from their burrows on Great Island, Newfoundland; as nighthawks dive and boom at dusk over a southern pine wood; and as Bobolinks sing their "song fantasia" in a grassy meadow bright with daisies and buttercups. Your spirits will be lifted.

Donald Kroodsma,
author of *The Singing Life of Birds*

Preface

Birds make a plethora of sounds, ranging in quality from musical whistles, resonant hoots, and sweet twitters, to nonmusical clicks, thumps, rattles, and churrs. The variety is astounding, and birds can be heard sounding off at all hours of the day and night, especially during the spring and summer breeding season. Our native birds are certainly noisy creatures, but why are they making all these sounds?

Nearly all bird sounds that we hear are communication signals that convey information to members of the same species, and sometimes even to other species. This is accomplished by the production of both vocal sounds (made with the aid of a voice box) as well as nonvocal sounds that are produced with wing feathers, the beak, or other anatomical structures. In the title of this book, the word "song" is used in a very general sense, referring to any significant sound a bird makes. Scientifically speaking, however, "song" usually refers to specific vocalizations made by songbirds, especially the musical singing of males used to attract mates and defend territories. Other vocalizations are referred to as "calls." For a technical discussion of these distinctions, refer to "All About Bird Sounds," on page 116. Also, for additional information, be sure to check out my support Web site: www.songsofwildbirds.com.

In this book, I share some of my most amazing recordings, gathered over many years as I traveled about the country to remote places where it was quiet enough to record. What might appear to be an odd assortment of birds is really the result of careful planning. Since I already introduced fifty common and well-known species in *Common Birds and Their Songs* (Houghton Mifflin, 1998), I was not concerned about including everyone's favorite bird. Instead, I chose species based on their story potential, on the sheer power of the sounds they make. This book gave me the chance to showcase recordings that I have not featured before: a chance to tell new stories and to have some fun.

Within the constraint of a short essay format, I include descriptions of experiences I've had in the field, along with historical references and quotes of poems and prose. In the essays, you will be introduced to a number of special kinds of bird songs, including flight songs, dawn and twilight songs, night songs, and courtship songs. You will encounter numerous examples of auditory interactions between individuals, such as countersinging, song-matching, duetting, and imitation. You'll learn about local dialects in bird songs. And you will be exposed to other unique and interesting sounds, such as nest-alarm calls, hawk-alarm calls, and the begging calls of young.

As you read through the essays, listen to the corresponding tracks on the compact disc. There, you will hear examples of what is discussed, accompanied by my narrated introductions to the recordings. Relax and enjoy the show — what better subject than the songs of wild birds!

About Sonagrams

Each essay includes a sound picture, or "sonagram," depicting a sound recording (or more than one recording) that is relevant to the essay. Technically referred to as a "sound spectrogram," the sonagram was developed for the scientific study of sounds. The physics behind the production of a sonagram is complex and will not be covered here, but the result is an intuitive graphical representation that roughly resembles the way we depict music on a musical staff. Refer to the example below. The horizontal axis of the sonagram represents time in seconds, while the vertical axis represents the pitch or frequency of the sound in kilohertz (kHz). One kHz is equivalent to 1,000 hertz (Hz) or 1,000 cycles per second (middle C on a piano is 440 Hz, while the highest key on a piano is 4,000 Hz or 4 kHz). In most cases, I simplify the frequency axis somewhat by including only one or two numbers that convey the dominant frequency or frequency range of a bird's song. In this book, bird sounds range from as low as 60 Hz (Ruffed Grouse drumming) to over 10 kHz (for certain notes in the European Starling's song).

Unlike the musical staff, which conveys notes of a particular pitch or frequency, the sonagram depicts everything from pure tones to nonmusical harsh sounds that cover a broad frequency range. Pure tones are recognizable as horizontal bands of limited width (e.g., the introductory note of the sparrow song pictured below). In contrast, broadband noises have a wide frequency span (e.g., the third and fifth sections of the song). Many bird songs include tonal elements that abruptly change in pitch, producing wavered notes or chips (e.g., the second and fourth sections of the song). Sound elements that are rapidly repeated might sound like a musical trill, a dry trill, a nonmusical rattle, or a buzz, depending on their frequency structure and repetition rate. While the reader is not expected to infer the quality of a bird's sound merely by looking at a sonagram, sound pictures do provide useful impressions and can be enjoyed in their own right, as graphic and artistic expressions of the sounds that birds make.

White-crowned Sparrow song

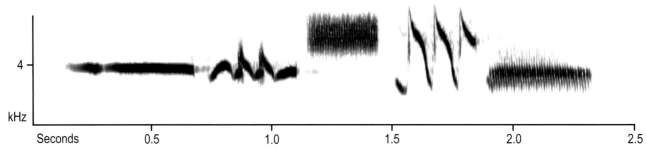

Northern Cardinal

The Compact Disc

The audio compact disc that accompanies this book has been carefully crafted to provide the reader with excellent examples of the bird sounds that are discussed in the essays. Each recording includes a brief narrated introduction. The tracks on the disc correspond to the fifty essay numbers, which can be found in the upper left corner of each essay page.

The Fifty Essays

Essay numbers correspond to track numbers on the compact disc.

1. Common Loon
2. Pied-billed Grebe
3. American Bittern
4. Bald Eagle & Red-tailed Hawk
5. Ruffed Grouse
6. Wild Turkey
7. Virginia Rail
8. Sandhill Crane
9. American Woodcock
10. Common Snipe
11. Atlantic Puffin
12. Mourning Dove
13. Great Horned Owl
14. Barred Owl
15. Eastern Screech-Owl
16. Common Nighthawk
17. Whip-poor-will & Chuck-will's-widow
18. Pileated & Ivory-billed Woodpeckers
19. Yellow-bellied Sapsucker
20. Eastern Wood-Pewee
21. Willow Flycatcher
    (& other *Empidonax* flycatchers)
22. Red-eyed Vireo
23. Blue Jay
24. Common Raven
25. Carolina Wren
26. Winter Wren
27. Blue-gray Gnatcatcher
28. Eastern Bluebird
29. American Robin
30. Wood Thrush
31. Hermit & Swainson's Thrushes
32. Thrush Flight Calls
33. Northern Mockingbird
34. European Starling
35. Black-throated Green Warbler
36. Ovenbird
37. Summer Tanager
38. Scarlet Tanager
39. Northern Cardinal
40. Rose-breasted Grosbeak
41. Grasshopper Sparrow
42. Henslow's Sparrow
43. White-crowned Sparrow
44. Bobolink
45. Brown-headed Cowbird
46. Red-winged Blackbird
47. Eastern & Western Meadowlarks
48. Baltimore Oriole
49. American Goldfinch
50. House Finch

Common Loon

"CRAZY AS A LOON" might well have described me, furiously paddling about in my small canoe in the black of night, trying to get close to several loons that were sounding off somewhere in the middle of the lake. On the advice of Dr. Judith McIntyre, who completed her Ph.D. on loon behavior at the University of Minnesota, I had traveled to Stillwater Reservoir in the Adirondack Mountains of upper New York, Judy's research base for more than twenty years. My hard work paid off. On that magical night in late July of 1988, I gathered loon recordings that remain among the best of my recording career.

The Common Loon has four primary vocalizations: the yodel, wail, hoot, and tremolo. The yodel is the breeding call of the species, given by males at the beginning of the breeding season to attract mates, primarily at night or during the twilight hours. Three melodic introductory notes are followed by wildly undulating calls that echo beautifully off the surrounding hills. The wail, given by both sexes, is reminiscent of the howl of a wolf. Wails indicate a willingness to interact with other loons. Another call is a simple hoot, a rarely heard soft note given by individuals in a group.

The expression "crazy as a loon" derives from yet another loon call: a weird tremulous utterance known as the tremolo. Likened to "maniacal laughter," the tremolo is the vocalization most likely to be heard during the day when humans encounter loons on their nesting grounds. Why is this? Because the tremolo is primarily a distress call indicating conflict or a desire to escape (although a special version of the tremolo may be given as an antiphonal duet between pairs in nonalarm situations). Canoers take note: you may hear tremolos and think the loons are laughing happily and saying hello. But now you know that this isn't so. The message is actually *Please go away* and let me tend my nest."

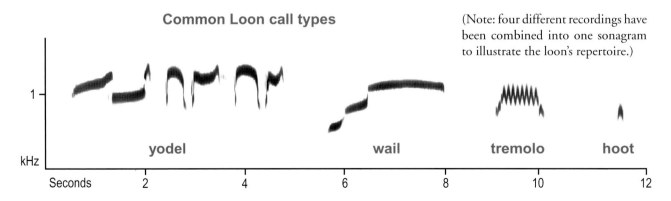

Common Loon call types

(Note: four different recordings have been combined into one sonagram to illustrate the loon's repertoire.)

yodel   wail   tremolo   hoot

Pied-billed Grebe

WHEN I BEGAN WRITING this book, my first impulse was to feature mostly songbirds, the pretty-looking and prettily singing birds that are familiar to all. But then I began thinking about which species really interested *me,* about what stories I would most enjoy telling. I made a quick list, and to my surprise, most were not songbirds at all. I wanted to talk about owls and rails, about critters that hoot and holler from thickets and marshes, or sound off in the dark of night, mystifying all who hear them. I wanted to tell about sounds that instantly capture one's attention and imagination and beg for identification. And so, I cannot help but wax poetic about one of the most marvelous wild sounds of our native freshwater marshes—the cuckoolike outburst of the Pied-billed Grebe, a small ducklike bird with a short "pied" (bicolored) beak that makes its living diving for fish, frogs, and invertebrates.

Commonly heard from marshes throughout most of the United States and southern Canada, the grebe's breeding or territorial song begins with soft *kuk* notes that quickly increase in speed and volume, followed by a long string of resonant *cow* or *kowp* calls, and often ending with a series of drawn-out notes that sound like a donkey braying. With throat distended, the singing bird bows down and submerges its breast while giving this remarkable display (see photograph).

Both sexes sing, but the female's version is softer and higher in pitch. Interestingly, the female often joins her mate to produce a special "song duet," which may include sections of antiphonal calling. Another common utterance is the "greeting call," a short outburst of staccato notes given during special courtship displays and often as a duet between the mates. I love the guttural calls of Pied-billed Grebes. For me, they are primeval voices of the marsh itself, exhalations of the mud and murk, bubbling forth through the throats of birds.

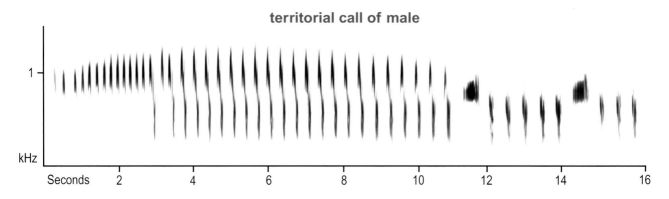

territorial call of male

1 kHz

Seconds 2   4   6   8   10   12   14   16

American Bittern

THE MOST UNUSUAL of all freshwater wetland sounds is perhaps the resounding territorial call of the male American Bittern. For many, it is a disembodied voice of northern marshes, a mysterious pumping sound that booms out of thick marsh vegetation — maybe the call of a giant frog, or the bellowing of the mythical Marsh King who makes his home deep in the swamp. How could a naive listener guess that the source of this unusual call is a stocky wading bird related to the herons and egrets?

Cryptically colored, the brown-streaked American Bittern usually stands motionless and blends right in with the cattails. But just before calling, he opens and closes his bill with rapid jerking motions, producing loud clicks as he gulps air to inflate his muscular esophagus. After several gulps, he begins his performance, repeatedly throwing his head and neck upward and forward in violent convulsive movements to produce a loud, resonant *oong-k'-choonk, oong-k'-choonk, oong-k'-choonk,* that can be heard a half mile or more across an open marsh. It is not surprising that the male's eerie breeding call has earned him several wonderfully descriptive common names, including "Water-Belcher," "Mire-Drum," "Stake-Driver," and, my favorite, "Thunder-Pumper."

I got my best recording one night in a huge North Dakota wetland. A bittern called occasionally from far out in the marsh. In pitch-black darkness I canoed toward the sound, following narrow waterways until I converged upon the source. Paddling through muck and grime, I managed to place my microphone within twenty feet of the caller. My hard work paid off. When dawn arrived, I got a recording that is the envy of bittern recordists the world over. I'm certain you will be impressed. I hereby call upon everyone to celebrate the bittern's resounding call, which some of our forefathers found so disturbing that they actually plotted to rid the marshes of this dreaded, evil bird. All hail the Thunder-Pumper, King of the Marsh!

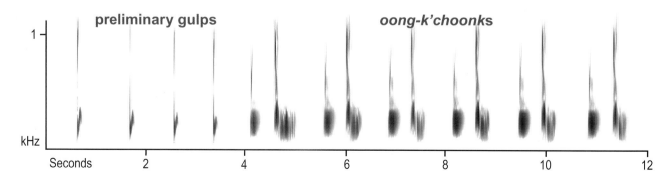

Bald Eagle & Red-tailed Hawk

WATCHING MOVIES as a child, I became familiar with the appearance and cry of the Bald Eagle, America's national bird, easily recognized by its white head and tail set against its dark brown body feathers. I was duly impressed by the eagle's penetrating call, so often heard in movies set in the Wild West. You've seen it and heard it, I'm sure: an eagle soaring high overhead, punctuating its glide with loud hissy shrieks, *kee-yeeer . . . kee-yeeer,* a chilling but familiar sound that seems perfectly fitting for such a fierce and noble bird.

Nice image, huh? Well, I hate to tell you, but this is all a *bunch of bunk*! Perhaps the movie people were ignorant. Or else they purposely conspired to confuse us. But the image they've perpetrated is just plain wrong. First of all, the eagle that is most likely to be seen soaring overhead in the American West is a different species, the Golden Eagle, an all-brown raptor that rarely calls in flight. And what of the shrieking cry? Well, that's actually the screech of the widespread Red-tailed Hawk or else its western relative, the Swainson's Hawk. Even if the bird in the movie were a Bald Eagle, you probably would never hear it shriek, because the Bald Eagle's primary call is not a shriek at all, but rather a simple chirp, described by ornithologist Arthur Cleveland Bent as "ridiculously weak and insignificant . . . quite unbecoming a bird of its size and strength." Naturalist William Brewster called it "a snickering laugh expressive of imbecile derision." Not what we'd expect from our national bird, is it?

Perhaps Ben Franklin was right after all. He argued that the cunning Wild Turkey should represent our fine nation, rather than the lowly Bald Eagle, which he considered to be "a bird of bad moral character," referring to its habit of eating carrion and other scraps of food. It's time to set the record straight. The Bald Eagle chirps like a big fat songbird. The Golden Eagle soars in silence. It is the Red-tailed Hawk who makes the hissy screech that many take to be the eagle's cry: *kee-yeeer . . . kee-yeeer.*

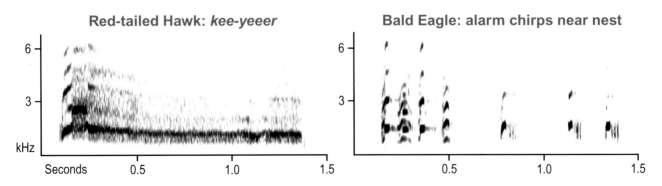

Red-tailed Hawk: *kee-yeeer*   **Bald Eagle: alarm chirps near nest**

Red-tailed Hawk

Ruffed Grouse

MOST MALE BIRDS attract mates and proclaim territories by singing with the help of a voice box—or syrinx—located in the windpipe just above the heart. But a variety of species augment vocal sounds by producing "mechanical communication signals," using portions of their anatomy to create sound. For instance, woodpeckers drum rapidly on resonant wood with their beaks to alert other woodpeckers of their whereabouts. And many hummingbirds court by flying rapidly to and fro, making high-pitched metallic sounds caused by air vibrating their stiff wing feathers. But, to me, the most amazing of all mechanical bird sounds is the drumming of the Ruffed Grouse, a chickenlike bird that inhabits deciduous and mixed forests from northern Georgia all the way to Alaska.

In the spring, male grouse perch on fallen logs in the forest, often arriving before dawn's light. The male begins his drumming display by bracing his tail, puffing up his breast, and ruffling his neck feathers. Then he opens and closes his wings in rapid succession, producing very low-pitched thumps at a frequency of only 60 Hz or cycles per second. The thumping starts out slow but quickly gains in speed, and the rapidly beating wings turn into a complete blur as the drumroll reaches its peak.

How on earth does the grouse produce such an unusual sound? Early investigators assumed that the thumps were caused by compression of air against the male's breast as the wings were suddenly drawn inward, like Tarzan beating on his chest. But this is incorrect: the thumps are actually little sonic booms created as air suddenly rushes to fill a vacuum made when the wings are thrust outward from the breast. Regardless of how the sound is made, grouse drumming is amazing to behold, a low-pitched marvel that is often felt more than it is heard.

(Note: grouse drumming is so low that you should listen with headphones or through big speakers; otherwise you may hear only the swish of feathers.)

drumming of a male Ruffed Grouse

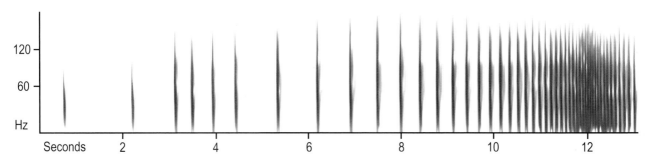

Wild Turkey

BENJAMIN FRANKLIN argued that the Wild Turkey should be our national bird, and his reasoning was sound. The turkey is an American icon. It was considered a noble bird and was an important staple in the diet of our European forefathers. The turkey roamed the deciduous forests and clearings in which Pilgrim settlements took root. Like humans, the turkey is a socially complex species and usually travels in groups. And the turkey is greatly respected by hunters for its exceptional intelligence and wary manner, making it difficult to hunt or capture. Ben's argument was powerful, but not powerful enough to convince fellow lawmakers, who thought the turkey looked silly, with its bald red head, and who were not impressed by its call, an incomprehensible gobbling befitting a fool.

The Wild Turkey is a true North American native. However, it was domesticated in Mexico and then quickly became established over much of the European world. Domestic turkeys are not as cunning as Wild Turkeys, and most strains have lost their beautiful iridescent colors. Our perception of the turkey as a noble bird has dwindled, alas, and in slang the word "turkey" has come to refer to a dimwitted buffoon—a far cry from the truth when it comes to the wild strain.

Turkeys make a variety of calls. The familiar gobble of the male is given with head thrown forward and neck feathers ruffled (main photo). Other calls include various yelps and clucks, some being contact notes and others expressions of alarm. When courting, the strutting male fans his tail, lowers his wings, and pulls his head back (inset). One sound accompanying the strut is the swish made as the male drags his wings along the ground. Another is a very low-pitched humming note preceded by a higher-pitched *chump*. Despite vast research on the species, biologists have never determined the source of the low hum. The disc features a variety of sounds, including yelps of females along with male gobbles, chumps, and hums, from a flock coming off its roost at dawn.

gobble of a male Wild Turkey

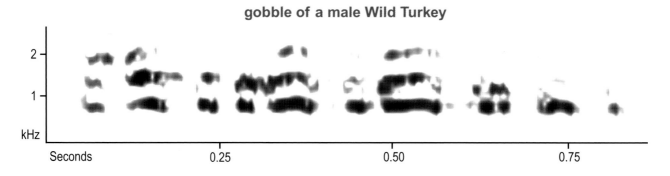

strutting posture

Virginia Rail

MY LOVE OF NATURE was evident by the time I was six years old. I wandered the forests and fields around my Missouri home, absorbed in all the natural wonders. I took particular delight in a nearby large lake, with a cattail marsh that I loved to explore. During one of my wetland expeditions, I spotted a small chickenlike bird walking along the muddy edge of the cattail stand and then disappearing into the thicket. It had a rusty red breast and red on its bill. I hurried home to my Peterson Field Guide in excited anticipation. Before long I had him identified: a Virginia Rail.

"Why do they call them rails?" I remember wondering. "Maybe something to do with railroads?" The answer came years later when I studied birds in an academic setting. It turns out that "rail" is derived from the French word *râle,* which refers to these secretive marsh birds and the moaning or scraping noises they make. There are six species in North America: the King Rail, Clapper Rail, Virginia Rail, Yellow Rail, Black Rail, and the Sora. All inhabit freshwater marshes except the Clapper Rail, which prefers saltmarsh habitats.

The sounds rails make, primarily at night, are diverse and unusual, ranging from plaintive whistles to clicks, clucks, and low-pitched grunts. The Virginia Rail has two major calls: a metallic *kick, kick, kidick, kidick, kidick,* given early in the breeding season by males to attract mates, and a descending series of grunting *oink*s that signify pair bonding. An amazing thing about the *oink* series is that it is often given as a duet, with male and female mates calling antiphonally during each outburst. The female's notes are higher in pitch than the male's. While recording Virginia Rails in the Adirondack Mountains, I was fortunate to capture several *oink* duets in full stereo. The splendid example on the compact disc allows you to hear the whereabouts of each bird, as well as its individual contributions to the duet.

grunting *oink* series of a Virginia Rail

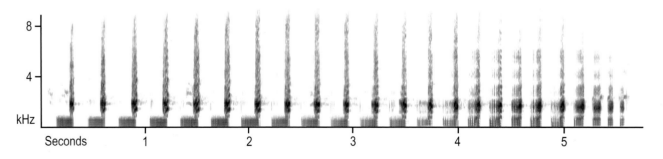

Sandhill Crane

IN JAPANESE LORE, cranes have long symbolized fidelity, prosperity, and longevity. More recently, origami paper cranes have become an international symbol of peace; but how did this come about? The answer lies with the story of Sadako Sasaki, a brave Japanese girl. Just two years old when the bomb fell on Hiroshima on August 6, 1945, Sadako initially survived, but her exposure to radioactivity brought on leukemia when she was eleven years old. While receiving treatment, she was reminded of the Japanese legend that if a sick person folded one thousand paper cranes, the gods might make him well again. Sadako began folding cranes and completed her task within a month, but nevertheless died several months later. Now, every year, students from all over the world fold cranes and send them to the Children's Monument in Hiroshima's Peace Park, in honor of Sadako.

Two crane species are found in North America: the rare Whooping Crane and the more numerous Sandhill Crane, recognized by its gray color and red cap. Most sandhills are migratory, and great numbers winter in the southern states, especially in southern Texas and New Mexico. Many also winter in Florida, and there is a resident population in the Southeast that is entirely nonmigratory. During the spring, migrating cranes move northward in large flocks, congregating along the way in places such as the Platte River in Nebraska. Their call is a loud trumpeting rattle, given in flight or on the ground.

Cranes mate for life but renew pair bonds each spring. During courtship, they "dance" by leaping into the air with wings spread while calling. Mated pairs hold their heads up and cross beaks before copulating. They maintain their bond by calling in unison—an exciting antiphonal duet combining the male's low-pitched call with the female's higher staccato note: *garuu-tucka-ruuu-tucka-ruuu-tucka*. The two unison call recordings on the compact disc were made at Okefenokee National Wildlife Refuge in southern Georgia and at Seney National Wildlife Refuge in upper Michigan.

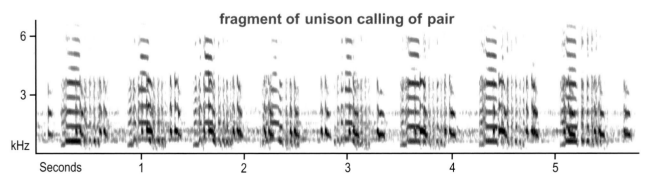

fragment of unison calling of pair

American Woodcock

IT WAS LATE MARCH when I first heard a woodcock sing. I was on a weekend outing with friends in the hills of West Virginia. After dark, we went for a long walk down an old farm road, surrounded by forest, fields, and pasture. A high-pitched twittering sound soon caught our attention; it came first from one direction, then from another, and finally passed directly overhead. Everyone was completely stumped. But after several minutes of listening, I became the star of the show when I suddenly blurted out "It's a woodcock!" Though I was unfamiliar with the bird, I based my identification on an essay I had read just days before in Aldo Leopold's conservation classic, *A Sand County Almanac* (1949).

In his unforgettable essay "Sky Dance," Leopold immortalized the spring breeding display of the American Woodcock, a plump, seemingly neckless bird with a long tapered beak. The silly-looking woodcock is a member of the shorebird family and frequents wet shrubby areas, where it feeds on earthworms by inserting its long flexible beak into worm holes.

As Leopold so elegantly described, the action begins at dusk when male woodcocks fly from their swampy hideouts to old farm fields. The male struts about on the ground, making nasal *peent* calls that resemble the calls of nighthawks (page 46). Then he takes flight and swiftly ascends in a series of wide spirals. Up and up he goes until he is a speck in the sky, silhouetted by the fading sunset. All the while he makes a high twittering sound, produced by air moving over narrow feathers on his wings. At the apex of his flight, he suddenly tumbles from the sky with erratic movements, as if a wing were broken. As he drops, he vocalizes—a sweet whimpering warble accompanies his descent. Then, just before hitting the ground, he levels off and glides back to his display site, where he resumes calling. He will breed with any female that approaches him. The show usually ends as darkness arrives, but when the moon is bright, the male woodcock may continue his remarkable display all through the night.

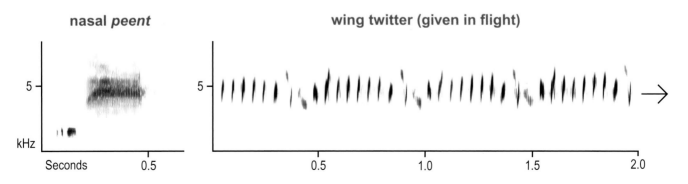

Common Snipe

AS A CUB SCOUT, I was introduced to the fine art of "snipe hunting" by my scout leaders. Along with other new recruits, I was taken deep into the forest and given a paper bag. I was told that snipe are flightless nocturnal birds about the size of a chicken and that if I quacked like a duck they would come running. To catch one, all I had to do was throw the bag over it. But, watch out . . . they have teeth! Imagine: a bunch of frightened eight-year-olds quacking in the woods at night, fully expecting toothed snipe to come running to our bags. Of course, this was all a *big* joke, a popular form of scout hazing in those days. The funny thing is, nobody in charge realized that snipe are real and that they are actually hunted in the South, not with a bag at night, but with shotguns during the day.

The Common Snipe, a member of the shorebird family, breeds in marshes across the northern United States and throughout most of Canada. A stocky bird with a long beak, the snipe resembles the American Woodcock (page 32), but has a stiff beak and more of a neck. Snipe make several sounds. On the wintering grounds, they give a raspy *scaipe* call when flushed. On their breeding grounds, they often perch and make a repeated, grinding *witcha-witcha-witcha-witcha,* often calling for minutes on end (see photo). But their most incredible sound is nonvocal—a tremulous winnowing given as they fly over their territories by day or night: *hu-hu-hu-hu-hu-hu-hu-hu.*

Also referred to as booming, this eerie sound is produced by the flow of air over outstretched tail feathers, modulated by beating of the wings. Henry David Thoreau immortalized the winnow in *Walden,* in the section entitled "Spring": "We need the tonic of wildness—to wade sometimes in marshes where the bittern and meadow-hen lurk, and hear the booming of the snipe." The calling bird (usually a male) flies in large circles and periodically swoops downward, spreading his tail feathers to produce the sound, which lasts about three seconds. My best recording of winnowing, featured on the disc, is from an Adirondack marsh, punctuated by frogs calling in the dark of the night.

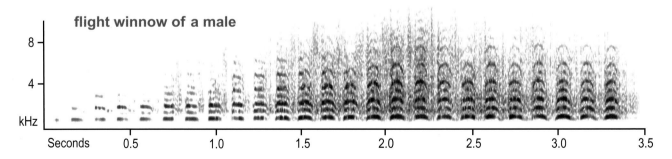

flight winnow of a male

Atlantic Puffin

"NO PUFFIN HERE," read a sign in a small restaurant along the coast of Maine. The sign featured a picture of a well-known seabird, the Atlantic Puffin, inside a red circle with a red slash across it. The sign had a double meaning. On the one hand, it was a silly-looking No Smoking sign, appropriate to a restaurant along the Maine coast where puffins are native. On the other hand, it symbolized the near extermination of puffins in the region in the late 1800s, due to hunting for meat, eggs, and feathers.

I was on my way to visit Dr. Stephen Kress, a National Audubon Society research biologist and director of the well-known Project Puffin. In 1973, Steve initiated efforts to restore puffins to historic nesting islands in the Gulf of Maine. He transported young puffins from a thriving population in Newfoundland to Eastern Egg Rock Island, where he raised them in artificial burrows and eventually established a stable breeding colony—a truly remarkable restoration success story. Steve gave me a personal tour of Eastern Egg Rock and then paved the way for a special expedition to Newfoundland, where I hoped to record the puffin's amazing call.

Two weeks later, I met seabird researchers Michael Rodway and Heidi Regehr at a dock not far south of Witless Bay, Newfoundland. A local fisherman boated us to Great Island, home of the largest breeding colony of puffins in North America, with an estimated 250,000 nesting in burrows in thick grassy turf at the top of the cliffs. Puffins are typically silent as they fly about, swim in the ocean, and perch on rocks. But they do vocalize from their burrows. Their surprising call is a moaning snore reminiscent of someone revving a chain saw. On Great Island, I placed my microphone near the entrance to a burrow and ran cable to our tiny research hut, hundreds of feet away. Inside, merrily sipping hot tea with Michael and Heidi, I captured superb recordings of the puffin's eminently expressive snore.

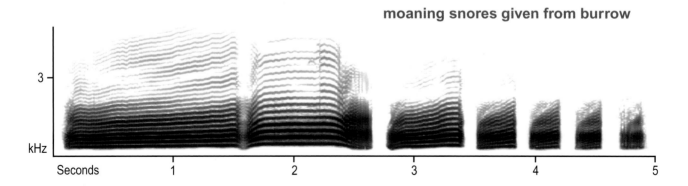

moaning snores given from burrow

Mourning Dove

WITH A BITTERSWEET mixture of shame and fond recollection, I remember how, as a young man, my friends and I would hunt doves in the autumn as flocks came to roost at dusk in shrubby tangles among the farm fields of northern Missouri. Truth be told, I remember that it was fun to blow the swift flyers from the sky. Chalk it up to youthful indiscretion and insensitivity, I guess, or to fascination with guns and power. But now, as an older man, I cannot imagine harming one of these beautiful creatures for any reason, unless perhaps hunger forced me to hunt to survive.

Sleek and fast-flying, the graceful Mourning Dove is abundant and widespread and is found throughout the United States and much of southern Canada. As well-known birds of yard and garden, doves frequent bird feeders and build platform nests of twigs and pine needles on limbs sheltered by leaves. A monogamous species, pairs often perch side by side and may be observed preening one another in what appears to be an expression of tender affection (note: scientists call this appeasement behavior and take exception to anthropomorphic descriptions indicating love or affection).

The Mourning Dove is named for its mournful-sounding song, heard during the spring and summer breeding season: *coo-uh-coooo-coo-coo*. Males inflate their throats when they sing and often coo from a prominent perch, such as a telephone wire. The song is primarily given by unmated males early in the breeding season (females occasionally give a faint version of the song). A shorter version of the song, *coo-uh-coooo*, is given by paired males to attract mates to nest sites. It is rarely heard once nesting commences. Mourning Doves also make a conspicuous nonvocal sound: a melodic twittering of their wings when they take flight or come in for a landing. Apparently, this sound is caused by movement of air over the wing feathers. Individuals seem to have control over the flight twitter, because doves sometimes take off or land silently.

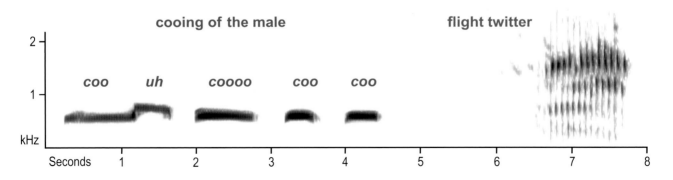

male cooing

Great Horned Owl

IN PASSAMAQUODDY LEGEND, a Great Horned Owl lures a young maiden with his "magical flute." She is so entranced by his melody that she allows him to carry her off to the village of the owls, where they marry and live happily ever after. Most other Native American tribes associated owls with evil or death. The Apache believed that owls were the embodied spirits of the dead. In his book *An Apache Campaign in the Sierra Madre* (1886), John Bourke tells how Apache scouts tracking Geronimo were terrified when they discovered that a U.S. soldier had a Great Horned Owl in his possession. They considered it a very bad omen and made the soldier leave the owl behind.

The Great Horned Owl ranges through most of the Americas, from the edge of the tundra in Alaska and Canada all the way south to Tierra del Fuego. In the United States, the species occupies nearly all regions and habitats, including eastern forests, deserts, prairies, high mountains, and the northern boreal forest. The word "horned" refers to the species' prominent "ear tufts," which have nothing to do with hearing, but rather are used in visual communication and for camouflage. One of our largest owls, the Great Horned has a wingspan approaching 60 inches and is capable of taking prey up to the size of a cat or small dog. It is the only predator that regularly eats skunks.

The Great Horned Owl makes a variety of sounds. The classic hoot, given by both sexes, is a low-pitched *hoo-h-hoo, hoo, hoo,* given all on one pitch. Although the female is larger than the male, her hoot is slightly higher in pitch. Great Horneds make several other sounds, including barks (adult alarm calls) as well as hissy screeches and whistles (immature begging calls). Every year I receive numerous inquiries about weird sounds of the night. Almost invariably the question goes like this: "All night long I heard bloodcurdling screeches coming from the woods around my house. What creature, pray tell, is making this sound?" And invariably the answer is: "immature Great Horned Owl."

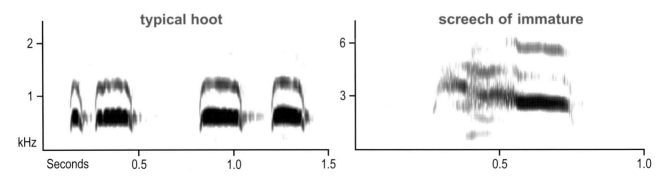

Barred Owl

A CHUNKY OWL with a round head, spots on its back, and streaks on its breast, the Barred Owl is perhaps the most familiar owl in eastern North America, or at least its call is familiar: a slurred series of hoots sounding like *hoo, hoo, hoo'ooo . . . hoo, hoo, hoo'oo-awl*, with the cadence of the popular memory phrase *Who cooks for you, who cooks for you-all?* Slightly smaller than the Great Horned Owl (page 40), the Barred Owl has a wingspan of about 42 inches and is capable of taking prey as big as a goose (although it feeds mostly on mice). The Cherokees have a legend explaining how the owl got its spots. Owl had a girlfriend he would go see every night, but he was embarrassed by his drab appearance and would hide in the shadows. Her parents and brothers wondered about this and the brothers decided to shed light on the problem. One night when Owl came to visit, the brothers suddenly threw sumac wood onto the fire, brightening the flames and throwing light on Owl. But this also threw sparks that landed on Owl's back and burned spots into his beautiful coat of brown feathers.

The Barred Owl has a large repertoire of sounds, including several variants on the hooting theme. Aside from the classic hoot series described above, there is (1) a simple *hoo-all*, (2) an ascending hoot series that ends with *hoo-awl*, (3) a spirited outburst with a pair hooting back and forth excitedly, like two monkeys going berserk with raucous maniacal calling, and (4) hissy screeches made by immatures begging for food. The female's hoot is higher in pitch than the male's. In his book *The Singing Life of Birds*, Donald Kroodsma presents evidence that female hoots can also be recognized by a slight vibrato added to the very end of their hoot series. While the male ends with a smooth *hoo-awl*, the female wavers her ending, producing a more throaty *hoo-awlllll*. This obvious sexual difference in the ending can be heard several times on the compact disc.

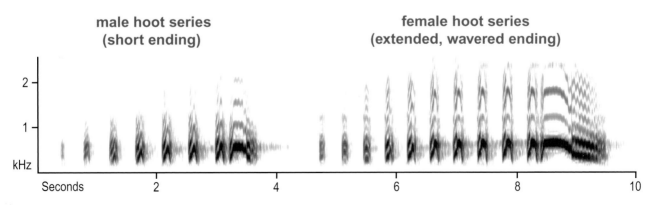

male hoot series (short ending)   **female hoot series (extended, wavered ending)**

Eastern Screech-Owl

FOR MANY YEARS, it was my opinion that Eastern Screech-Owls do not screech. This is because their two main calls are trills that scarcely resemble a screech (see below). However, after speaking recently with Gary Ritchison, professor of biology at Eastern Kentucky University and author of several scientific studies of screech-owls, I have changed my mind. Apparently, if you stumble on a screech-owl nest at night (they nest in tree hollows or human-made nest boxes), the parent owls will dive at you, screeching loudly and snapping their bills in protest, leaving you with an indelible memory of the event. This has never happened to me, but it did happen to fellow recordist Wil Hershberger, who has provided the superb examples of alarm screeches presented on the compact disc.

The Eastern Screech-Owl ranges throughout the eastern half of the United States. It is a small owl, about 9 inches long, and has prominent ear tufts. Screech-owls come in two color varieties: a gray morph and a red morph (both morphs are pictured). They are found in diverse forest habitats and are the most common owls in suburban and urban woodlots.

The screech-owl has two main calls: a low-pitched melodic trill that is all on one pitch (the tremolo or bounce call, also called the monotonic trill), and an eerie, wavering trill that descends in pitch (the whinny call). The whinny is unforgettable. Some liken it to the scream of a terrified woman. It is thought to be a territorial defense song. In contrast, the tremolo is a pair or family contact call. Interestingly, members of a pair often "duet" by alternating tremolo calls. The female's trill is higher in pitch than the male's. The featured stereo recording, depicting what appears to be two pairs duetting at their territorial boundary, is the work of Dan Gibson, Canadian nature recordist and founder of the Solitudes series of nature and music productions. Dan's recording is beautiful beyond compare.

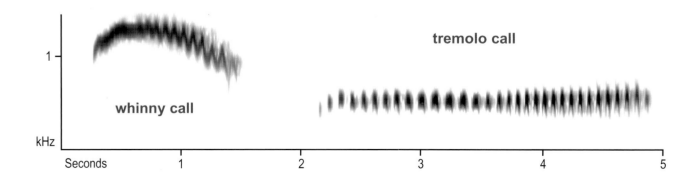

gray morph

Common Nighthawk

A HUGE FLOCK OF hawklike birds, numbering in the hundreds, wheeled about in the sky high above a small Ohio town at dusk in early September, drawing attention to themselves with occasional *peent* calls as they snatched insects from the air. The nighthawks are migrating! It was too noisy to record, so I leaned against my car with binoculars to my eyes, entranced by their aerial antics as they gradually moved out of sight to the south, silhouetted against the orange-red sky.

Found throughout North America, the nighthawk is named for its appearance when flying—its slender, knifelike wings resemble those of some small hawks. The nighthawk is not actually a night bird. Rather, it feeds during the twilight hours, and on occasion in the middle of the day. In the South, Common Nighthawks are sometimes called "bullbats" because of their erratic batlike flight and their courtship "boom" (see below), which faintly resembles the bellow of a bull. The nighthawk is a member of the nightjar family—one of its closest relatives is the Whip-poor-will (page 48). Nighthawks nest on barren areas in a variety of habitats and lay their eggs directly on the ground. They have also adapted to nesting on flat gravel roofs in urban areas. Nighthawks winter in South America and have one of the longest migration flights of any North American bird.

The male nighthawk has a spectacular courtship display. At dusk and dawn he circles above his nesting territory, giving characteristic nasal *peent* calls that sound similar to the notes of the American Woodcock (page 32). At regular intervals, he dives from the sky and then, just before hitting the ground, swoops upward with a *peent* accompanied by a muffled boom or *whoooof*, produced by air rushing through his wing feathers. After continuing this dramatic display for a number of minutes, he finally alights on the ground near his mate, fans his tail, puffs his throat, and wags from side to side, all the while croaking *auk, auk, auk* as the female watches in silence. Nighthawk courtship seems ancient and primeval, as if voicing the deep inner rumblings of the earth itself.

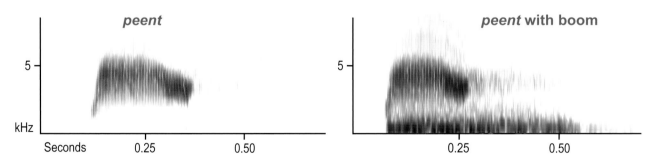

Whip-poor-will & Chuck-will's-widow

AD INFINITUM is Latin for "without end," meaning "to infinity, endlessly, without limit." For me, this phrase perfectly describes the Whip-poor-will's night singing. It seems to go on forever: *whip-poor-will, whip-poor-will, whip-poor-will, whip-poor-will* . . . ad infinitum. Early settlers were impressed by the repetitious song, which at first is pleasing, but after a while can become rather maddening, especially if a whip-poor-will is singing nearby. Some thought the song good luck, others bad luck. Some felt the song happy, others sad. I personally like Louis J. Halle's sensitive and poetic description of the song as "a steady pulsation of sound, like something organic in the earth itself, like the beating of one's own heart" (from his book *Spring in Washington,* first published in 1947).

The Whip-poor-will is a forest dweller found over much of the East, but it is absent from the southern states except in winter. There is also a Central American population that ranges northward into Arizona and New Mexico. The song of western birds has a noticeable burry quality. Whip-poor-wills are members of the nightjar family—nightjars the world over are active at night, and most have loud and distinctive night songs, often with a jarring quality. Whip-poor-wills feed on night-flying insects, which they catch on the wing with the aid of long whiskers protruding from the edges of the mouth. They feed mostly at dusk and dawn, or all night during moonlit periods. They are often encountered sitting on gravel roads in forested areas at night, their large eyes reflecting bright red in the headlights. Stop and watch, and you may see one flutter upward to catch a flying insect.

In the South, the larger and chunkier Chuck-will's-widow replaces the Whip-poor-will. Its four-part song is accented on the second and third syllables, *Chuck-WILL-WID-ow,* while the Whip-poor-will's three-part song is accented on the first and third syllables: *WHIP-poor-WILL.* Songs of both species are included on the compact disc.

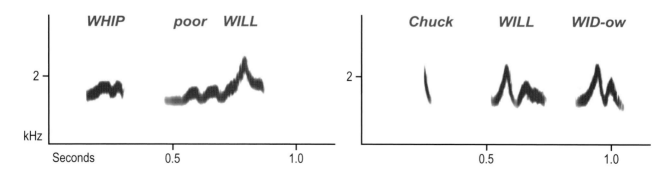

Chuck-will's-widow

18

Pileated & Ivory-billed Woodpeckers

GIANT WOODPECKERS leave lasting impressions. During my visit to the National Zoo in Washington, D.C., a Pileated Woodpecker actually landed on the hood of my car. I was stunned by his prehistoric, pterodactyl-like appearance. With a prominent crest and a huge chisel-shaped beak, he measured almost 19 inches long. The regal Ivory-billed Woodpecker, a species that until recently was thought to be extinct, may grow to nearly 21 inches long. A huge woodpecker by all counts, but not the largest in the world — that honor goes to the probably extinct Imperial Woodpecker of Mexico, which measures a whopping 24 inches!

The Pileated Woodpecker inhabits mature forested areas throughout the East. In Canada, it ranges from the Maritime Provinces westward to the Pacific Coast and south to California. Should you spot a giant woodpecker in the forest, it is almost certain to be a Pileated. The extremely rare Ivory-billed Woodpecker has a much more restricted distribution, though it formerly inhabited bottomland swamp forests throughout the South; it was thought to be extirpated because of logging. Recent confirmed sightings (along with video footage and tape recordings) offer compelling evidence that the Ivory-bill survives, but only in the virgin forests of the Big Woods region of eastern Arkansas. There, a huge research effort is under way, spearheaded by the world-famous Cornell Laboratory of Ornithology.

The calls of the two species are easy to tell apart. The Pileated's primary call is a boisterous, laughlike outburst of six to eight notes that drops in pitch at the end — it reminds me of the trademark laugh of Woody Woodpecker of television fame. In contrast, the Ivory-bill's call is a weak, nasal *kent* that sounds like the toot of a little tin horn. The drums of the two species also differ. The Pileated gives an even drumroll that fades at the end, whereas the Ivory-bill produces a simple "double-knock." Vocalizations of both species are featured on the disc.

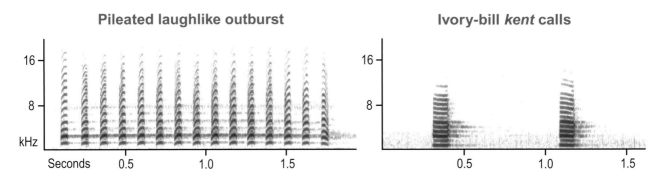

Pileated laughlike outburst   **Ivory-bill *kent* calls**

Ivory-billed Woodpecker

19

Yellow-bellied Sapsucker

A SAPSUCKER IS a type of woodpecker. There are four species in North America, of which three are very closely related: the Yellow-bellied Sapsucker of northern areas, the Red-naped Sapsucker of the mountain states, and the Red-breasted Sapsucker of Pacific coastal forests. These sapsuckers were long considered members of the same species but have recently been given full species status. Sapsuckers get their name from their habit of pecking tree bark to create "sap wells" arranged in spaced rows or columns. Sapsuckers eat the exposed inner bark and also drink the watery sap that fills the pits. They don't actually suck sap, but rather use their tongue to lap up the fluid. In light of this, world-famous bird expert Lang Elliott proposes that the common name be changed to something more accurate, like Yellow-bellied Sap*lapper,* rather than Sap*sucker*—their tongue is not a straw!

The sapsucker's sound repertoire includes a variety of calls. A simple mewing *waah* indicates mild disturbance. Hawklike squealing notes, *wee-yah, wee-yah, wee-yah,* are thought to be territorial calls. And a squeaking *weeka-weeka-weeka* accompanies social interactions. But the most interesting sapsucker sound is not a vocalization. It is the mechanical drumming sound made as males pound their beaks against resonant limbs to stake out territories at the beginning of the breeding season.

Most woodpeckers produce a rapid drumroll on an even tempo, and the drums of different species are often difficult to tell apart. Sapsuckers, however, are unique because they drum with an uneven tempo. A typical drum for the Yellow-bellied Sapsucker begins with a brief drumroll followed by an irregular series of couplets or single taps: *rattatatta, t-tat, t-tat, t-tat, t-tat,* with considerable variability in duration and timing. Sapsuckers will drum on anything that "sounds good," including gutters on houses, telephone poles, and metal boats. When I lived in the Adirondacks, a sapsucker used to rattle my brain each morning by drumming on a metal sign just outside my cabin. His irreverent banging is immortalized on the compact disc.

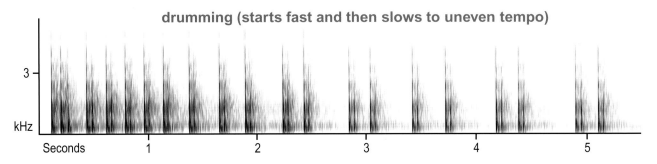

drumming (starts fast and then slows to uneven tempo)

20

Eastern Wood-Pewee

TRANQUIL AND CALMING, the plaintive notes of the Eastern Wood-Pewee have been variously described as sweet, pure, peaceful, serene, and sad. The pewee's daytime song is composed of two slurred, whistled phrases—a wavering *pee-a-wee* and a downward *pee-oh*. Delivery of these phrases is leisurely, with long pauses of five or ten seconds between. The *pee-a-wee* phrase is usually given more frequently, with the down-slurred phrase added every so often, as if to provide a sense of musical completion to the sequence: *pee-a-wee . . . pee-a-wee . . . pee-a-wee . . . pee-oh . . .*

Wintering in South America, the pewee is a late migrant, returning to its eastern deciduous forest habitat in mid-May, after the leaves have unfolded and the woods are vibrant green. The pewee is small and inconspicuous, and both sexes wear a coat of somber colors, with a dark olive-gray back and a light gray breast. Were it not for their songs, pewees would go largely unnoticed, as they spend most of their time high in the trees, where they perch on dead limbs and sally forth to catch flying insects.

While the leisurely daytime song is familiar to most birders living within the species' range, the male pewee also sings a special version of song for about a half hour at the break of dawn and sometimes at dusk. Animal psychologist Wallace Craig was the first to describe this behavior in his well-known 1926 study, "The Twilight Song of the Wood Pewee: A Preliminary Statement." In the twilight song, the singing rate is much faster than in normal song, with only one or two seconds' pause between phrases. Also, an entirely new phrase, sounding like *ahh-d-dee,* is added to the sequence. It is composed of notes that rise in pitch. A typical twilight song sequence might go like this: *pee-a-wee . . . ahh-d-dee . . . pee-oh . . . pee-a-wee . . . ahh-d-dee . . . pee-oh,* and so forth. If you want to hear the pewee's spirited twilight performance, locate a singing male during the day and then return the next morning before first light. Find a comfortable log to sit on. Listen for the first plaintive *pee-a-wee.* The male will sing leisurely at first, but before long he'll be piping his twilight notes at full tilt.

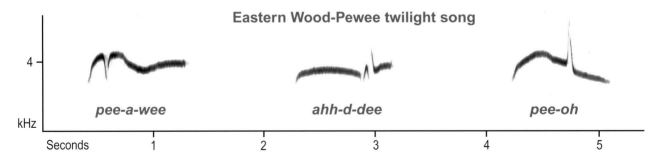

Eastern Wood-Pewee twilight song

pee-a-wee   *ahh-d-dee*   *pee-oh*

21

Willow Flycatcher

(& other *Empidonax* flycatchers)

THE BANE OF many bird watchers is a group of flycatchers in the genus *Empidonax*. Eleven species are found in North America, and all of them are small olive-colored birds that look very much alike. Aside from paying attention to range, the best way to identify the various "empids" is to learn their distinctive songs, which as a rule are unmusical and brief. But don't think this is going to be easy!

Five *Empidonax* make their homes in the East. The Willow Flycatcher (pictured) frequents dry brushy areas and says *fitz-bew*. The Alder Flycatcher prefers swamps and sings a song that sounds like *fee-bee-o*. The Acadian Flycatcher of mature deciduous woodlands sounds like *pit-seet*. The Least Flycatcher of open forest sings a dry, snappy *che-bek*. And the Yellow-bellied Flycatcher of the north woods sings *killik* or else *chu-wee*. Got that? To further confuse matters, let's add the western empids: The Western Flycatcher says *whee-seet*, the Gray goes *chi-wip*, the Dusky goes *sillit*, the Hammond's says *si-dit*, and the Buff-breasted says *pi-wit*. Easy to keep straight, huh? It's difficult enough just to learn the five eastern species! And good luck to those who try to tackle their calls. How on earth can one master the subtle differences between a *pit, wit, whit, peek, peet, seet,* or *breet*? Perhaps an exercise in frustration for all but the most dedicated birders!

The bird in the photograph was not singing at first, yet I knew instantly that it was a Willow Flycatcher because it was perched in a willow shrub. Likewise, Alder Flycatchers always perch in alder shrubs, Least Flycatchers in least shrubs, Acadian Flycatchers in acadia shrubs, and Yellow-bellied Flycatchers in yellow-bellied shrubs. And if you believe this nonsense, you must be perched in a gullible shrub!

(Note: five different recordings have been combined into one sonagram to illustrate the calls of the five species.)

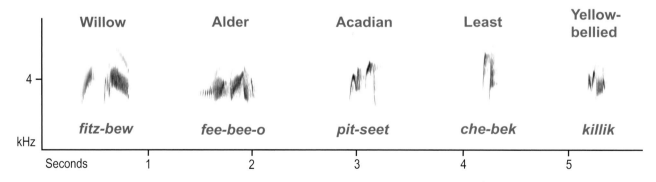

22

Red-eyed Vireo

A SMALL DRAB BIRD with a narrow pointed beak, the Red-eyed Vireo of our eastern deciduous forests and Canadian north woods is a common denizen of the treetops. Its claim to color is the red iris of its eye, but how often do we get close enough to see it? Actually, the Red-eyed is perhaps better known for its song. Males sing all day long, tirelessly repeating brief whistled song phrases with short pauses between: *see-wee . . . see-it . . . seedle-ee . . . see-o-wit . . . see-yer . . .* etc.

Arthur A. Allen, founder of the Cornell Laboratory of Ornithology, narrated an endearing description of the Red-eyed's singing pattern in his classic LP *Songbirds of America in Color, Sound, and Story* (1954): "As we leave the garden and walk along under the elms and maples by the roadside, we gradually realize there are birds singing overhead, furnishing background for all the other species . . . they are the Red-eyed Vireos, and high in the trees, they are more difficult to see than to hear. One bird singing by itself seems to say: *look up, way up, tree top, see it,* and so forth, without ever stopping." A popular nickname for the Red-eyed is "Preacher Bird," reflecting the male's habit of singing incessantly, almost without pause, like an overzealous preacher who doesn't know when to shut up.

Louise de Kiriline Lawrence, a Canadian ornithologist, followed a male through an entire day on May 27, 1952, and found that he sang a whopping 22,197 songs! Quite an accomplishment for any bird. The Red-eyed surely gets a prize for quantity of song, but the quality of his discourse seems mediocre at best, at least compared to the melodic and highly variable songs of a number of other species. The Red-eyed is perhaps like some people I know: he talks nonstop but doesn't have much to say. Actually, this isn't quite true. Studies reveal that each male has about 40 different songs. They all sound much the same to our ears, but a vireo can probably discern minor differences with ease. When you next hear a Red-eyed, listen for a unique song phrase, and then see if the male repeats it every forty songs or so.

Red-eyed Vireo song sequence

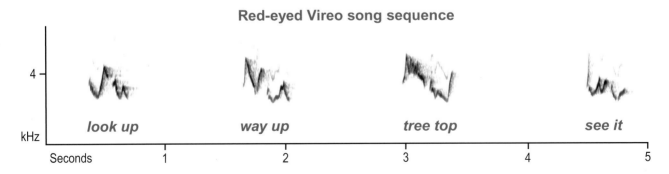

23

Blue Jay

NOISY AND BOISTEROUS, the Blue Jay makes his presence known with raucous calls and an aggressive disposition, especially at bird feeders, where his arrival causes most other songbirds to flee to a safe perch. His colors are a brilliant mix of blue, black, and white. He has a prominent crest, which he raises when he calls. Throughout eastern and central North America, the Blue Jay's range is expanding, with nestings reported as far west as Wyoming and even British Columbia.

Jays are highly social and often gather in noisy groups. The sexes look identical, making it very difficult to study social behavior and determine the functions of calls. The Blue Jay has an extremely varied vocabulary, an immense repertoire of sounds that tend to grade into one another. Precise categorization seems impossible, though sounds can be artificially lumped into several prominent groups.

First are the vibrant nasal *jay* or *jeer* calls, sometimes given as a two-part *jay-jay* or *jee-arr*. These grade into more musical calls variously described as sounding like *tull-ull, twirl-erl, tweedle,* or *whee-oodle,* and which are almost always accompanied by rhythmic bobbing movements. Then there are various squeaking calls resembling the sounds of a rusty pump handle or a squeaky gate. As family groups move about, they make soft nasal notes sounding like *queu-queu-queu.* Add to these an odd rattling call given only by females. In addition, Blue Jays imitate the sounds of certain hawks and have been known to fool expert birders into thinking a hawk is nearby. There is even a songlike sequence of soft clicks, whirrs, whines, and liquid notes. To convey the incredible variety, I've taken all my jay recordings and those of friends and arranged them on the disc to show how huge the jay's repertoire really is. I think you will agree that the Blue Jay deserves a Grammy Award for his outstanding vocal versatility!

several Blue Jay call types

(Note: four different recordings have been combined into one sonagram to illustrate the four call types.)

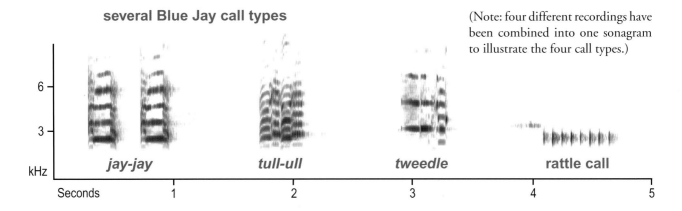

24

Common Raven

IN THE BEGINNING, according to Inuit myth, Tulugaq (Raven) flew about in darkness surrounded by nothing but falling snow. As snow gathered on his wings, Raven became playful and made a snowball, tossing it into the air. As the snowball fell through space, it gathered more and more snow, growing large enough for Raven to land upon it. Thus Raven created the world. But it was a dark world and Raven himself was colorless. So Raven stole light from a greedy old man who kept it hidden in a box in a dark hut, and he escaped by flying up through a smoke-hole. In the process, the smoky soot turned Raven's feathers black, a small price to pay for bringing light into the world.

The Common Raven is a cosmopolitan species found on all continents across the Northern Hemisphere. In North America, ravens range from the arctic tundra south to the western mountain states and beyond into Mexico. Absent from the central United States, they are found in the Northeast and in the Appalachian Mountains south to Georgia. They are known for their majestic flight and the spectacular aerial acrobatics they perform during courtship. Shy and wary in the wild, ravens may act rather tame as they scavenge for food near human habitations.

Ravens are exceedingly vocal and make an impressive variety of sounds. Their primary call is a hoarse, throaty *crawww* delivered as a loud croak or else with soft and delicate inflection. They also produce resonant bell-like tones, a hollow *haw-haw-haw-haw,* peculiar gulping sounds, a rattle resembling the drum of a woodpecker, and other bizarre utterances. Scientists have defined at least 20 different categories of sounds. Yet the functions of calls are not clearly understood, a matter complicated by the endless variation and intergradation between types. No matter what their meanings, raven vocalizations are a marvel, and they tend to bring a smile to one's face. Ravens seem a lot like people — they are wonderfully comic and expressive, but tend to make "much ado about nothing."

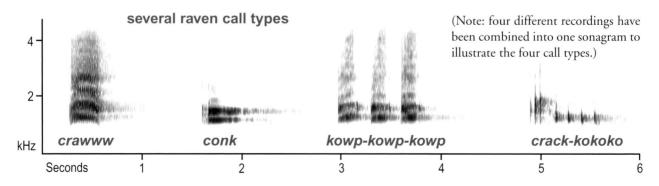

several raven call types

(Note: four different recordings have been combined into one sonagram to illustrate the four call types.)

crawww   *conk*   *kowp-kowp-kowp*   *crack-kokoko*

25

Carolina Wren

AS A GRADUATE STUDENT at the University of Maryland, I took a course in animal behavior taught by Eugene S. Morton, an ornithologist stationed at the National Zoo in nearby Washington, D.C. Gene was studying the vocal behavior of the Carolina Wren, and one of his prized research subjects was a female wren that he had named Buttercup. For a short while, Buttercup lived in a plush, well-furnished cage in the basement of the research building at the zoo. There she revealed an abundance of secrets about the vocal behavior of the species.

The Carolina Wren is a common eastern songbird, equally at home in backyard habitats and the wild woods. Year-round residents, males may be heard singing anytime during the year, although most singing occurs during the spring and early summer breeding season. The whistled song of the male is loud and ringing, composed of several rapidly repeated phrases that sound like *tea-kettle, tea-kettle, tea-kettle,* or *whiddy-you, whiddy-you, whiddy-you.* Males have about thirty different song types. Song output is greatest at dawn, when males switch song types every fifteen or so songs.

Carolina Wrens have a variety of calls. Gene defined at least twelve, describing them as *cheer, ti-dink, dit, rasp, chirt, chatter, pi-zeet, scee, pee, growl, nyerk,* and *tsuck.* It gets even more complicated, because many grade from one into another. Chatter calls are particularly interesting. A female typically chatters when threatening another female, and also when her mate sings aggressively during encounters with a neighboring pair. In the latter situation, the female generally overlaps her chatter with his song, contributing to an "aggressive duet" that many birders hear, but probably don't interpret correctly. Gene Morton has graciously provided me with an excellent recording of duetting behavior, featuring his beloved Buttercup, chattering in response to the songs of her mate.

duetting: male song followed by female chatter

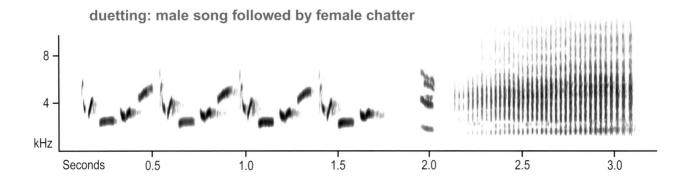

26

Winter Wren

CHIPMUNK BEHAVIOR was the focus of my master's degree research, which I undertook in the Adirondack Mountains of upstate New York. I didn't know much about birds, but when I began my field study in early May of 1973, I was immediately struck by the liquid ramble of high tinkling notes from a singer that inhabited a stand of spruce and fir near my camp. It was several days before I finally spied the little brown musician, perched atop a snag among the conifers, singing excitedly with tail cocked straight up—a Winter Wren. Ranging from the northern conifer woods of Maine and the Maritime Provinces across Canada to the Pacific coastal forests, Winter Wrens also are found at high altitudes in the Appalachian Mountains, as far south as Georgia.

Albert R. Brand, author of *Songs of Wild Birds* (1934), lauded the Winter Wren's bubbly song: "Each person has his own preference as to which woodland voice is the most beautiful. My choice is the Winter Wren. For beauty and joyfulness, to me, this is our finest sylvan sound." The song reminded John Burroughs of "a tremulous, vibrating tongue of silver," and Thoreau considered it "an exceedingly brisk and lively strain" that sounds like a "fine corkscrew stream issuing with incessant lisping tinkle from a cork, flowing rapidly."

The song of the Winter Wren is easy to recognize no matter where it is heard, but males from different parts of the continent sing noticeably different songs. Lasting five or six seconds, the songs of eastern birds are melodic and consist of about one hundred distinct notes. In contrast, the songs of western males last about seven seconds, sound very percussive, and contain more than two hundred notes, which are delivered in a rapid blur. Given this difference, it is not surprising that the ornithologist Don Kroodsma, who studied the Winter Wren's song in great detail, thinks that the eastern and western populations represent two different species. Listen to the examples on the compact disc, and see if you agree.

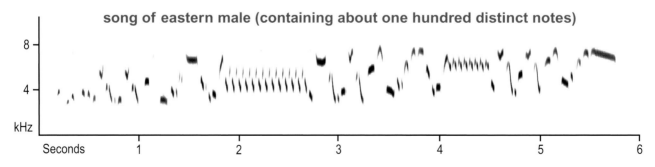

song of eastern male (containing about one hundred distinct notes)

27

Blue-gray Gnatcatcher

IN CELEBRATION OF DELICACY, I bring attention to a tiny gray bird whose main claim to fame in the world of bird sound is his fussy nasal calls, so evident to birders who frequent his domain. I'm referring to the Blue-gray Gnatcatcher, a widespread species found in wooded or shrubby areas throughout much of the United States, though absent from the northern prairie and northwestern mountain regions. Gnatcatchers seem equally at home in eastern deciduous forest, southern pine-oak woods, and even southwestern desert scrublands. They look like miniature mockingbirds.

The Blue-gray Gnatcatcher does not have a song in the conventional sense. In other words, males don't awaken each morning and pour forth well-defined melodic phrases that help them define their territories, find a mate, and maintain a pair bond. Or at least I don't think they do. Early in the nesting season, individuals do call excitedly at dawn, giving repeated nasal *zeee* or *speee* notes in a regular sequence that may last for many minutes. Is this a kind of song? Scientists think maybe it is, but they don't know for sure. And the fact that the sexes look almost identical makes study difficult.

To complicate matters, gnatcatchers have another utterance that definitely sounds like song, but that is not sung regularly, as songs usually are. Referred to as "complex song," it is a delicate ramble of squeaks, whistles, and mews that is reminiscent of the song of a catbird, but is delivered more rapidly and at a higher pitch. Sometimes imitations are thrown in, including notes and phrases resembling those of Blue Jay, American Crow, Tufted Titmouse, and Rufous-sided Towhee. Complex song is difficult to hear beyond a hundred feet or so, and it is easily overlooked. This makes me like it even more. In fact, I'm totally entranced by the gnatcatcher's delicate refrain. It is so sweet to my ears that whenever I hear it, I become fully absorbed in every little note coming from the mouth of the little gray muse.

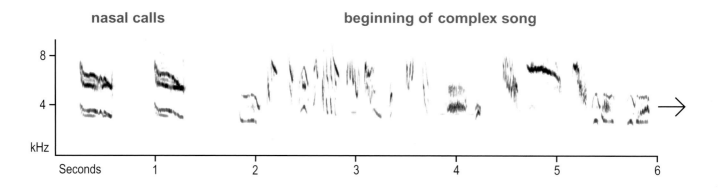

nasal calls   **beginning of complex song**

28

Eastern Bluebird

WHEREVER ONE TRAVELS in North America, there is a bluebird to delight the eye. In the East it is the Eastern Bluebird. In the West it is either the Western Bluebird or the Mountain Bluebird. All inhabit open areas and seem to evoke a cheerful mood. I grew up among the farmlands of northern Missouri, and bluebirds were my mother's favorite bird. The bluebird is the official state bird of New York, Missouri, Nevada, and Idaho. People put up nest boxes to attract them. People love bluebirds.

The song of the Eastern Bluebird is a delight to the ear, a series of bright, musical warbled phrases sounding like *cheer . . . cheerily . . . churee . . . cheer-cheerful-charmer.* Males have a repertoire of about fifty different song phrases, though differences are often subtle. At dawn, especially in areas where bluebirds are concentrated, males sing an excited song series that includes lots of sharp *chit* notes. They may even sing in flight as they move from perch to perch. The dawn performance is brief, lasting twenty minutes or less, and many bluebird enthusiasts are actually unaware of its existence. The presence of *chit* notes, which are usually given in alarm situations, betrays the high level of arousal among competing males during the dawn song melee. The female also occasionally sings, which is quite unusual among temperate-zone songbirds, but hers is a simpler song, usually given when predators are near the nest.

Bluebird song is a pleasure to behold, but what excites me most is the bluebird's singular call note: a sweet, vibrant *tru-lee* or *turalee.* Henry David Thoreau considered this call to be the premier sign of spring. When conditions were right, he felt that the environs called forth the sound, that on certain days in late winter or spring, the air over a field becomes "a foundry full of moulds for casting bluebird's warbles." I remember hearing this wonderful call while playing golf one April with a friend. At the height of my backswing, I heard the *tru-lee* of a bluebird flying overhead. I was so affected that I completely missed the ball. Needless to say, my friend had a *tru-lee* good laugh!

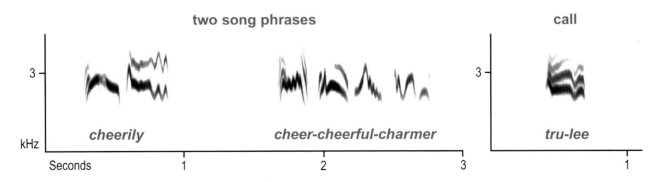

two song phrases   call

cheerily   *cheer-cheerful-charmer*   *tru-lee*

29

American Robin

A BROAD-WINGED HAWK glided across the yard in front of the little cabin in northern Michigan, flew into the pines, and landed on a limb. Simultaneously, I heard thin, high-pitched whistles coming from somewhere behind me: *seeeeeee . . . seeeeeee . . . seeeeeee.* I turned and aimed my parabolic microphone in the direction of the source and soon spied an American Robin perched on a high limb, its beak opening in concert with the calls. The hawk flew away, but I still managed to record this jewel of the robin's vocal repertoire: the little-known "hawk-alarm" call. Apparently, this call alerts other robins as well as other songbirds to the presence of an aerial predator. Ornithologist Peter Marler has studied such calls in other birds. He suggests that a number of songbird species the world over have developed hawk-alarm calls that follow the same general pattern: high-pitched drawn-out tones that prove difficult for a hawk (or a recordist) to localize. I felt blessed to get an excellent recording of the robin's manifestation of this call.

The American Robin needs little introduction. This widespread and abundant species is familiar to nearly everyone. And so is its song, a rollicking series of liquid, whistled phrases sounding like *cheerily, cheeriup, cheerio, cheerily,* rising and falling in pitch and with distinct pauses between each group of phrases. At dawn, robins sing an excited version of the song that lacks these typical pauses and includes soft flutey notes not found in normal song. There is even a "whisper song" composed primarily of the flutey sounds. Calls include a sharp *peek* and a throaty *tut,* given when ground predators, including people, come close to the nest: *peek . . . peek . . . tut, tut . . . peek . . . tut, tut.* Another common call sounds like the whinny of a horse—it signifies mild alarm. Quite a diversity of sounds from our yard and garden friend. But for me, it is the hawk-alarm whistle that is the robin's most special utterance. It is a call that is chock-full of meaning, telling us that a hawk is perched somewhere nearby.

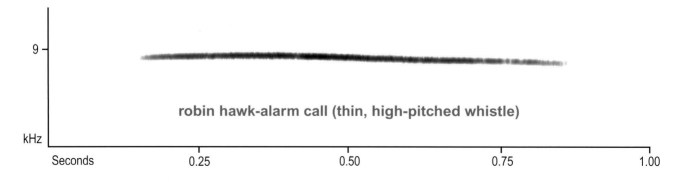

robin hawk-alarm call (thin, high-pitched whistle)

30

Wood Thrush

I FELL IN LOVE with Wood Thrushes while living in Washington, D.C. For relaxation, I often walked the wooded trails of a park near my Georgetown apartment. Wood Thrushes were abundant and graced the city woodlot with superb vocal performances. Especially at dusk, males would duel each other with song, singing back and forth energetically, as if showing off their favorite tunes before calling it quits for the night. I was awestruck by their music—ethereal notes full of magic and repose.

As denizens of the eastern deciduous forest, Wood Thrushes range from the southern states north into Canada. To my dismay, Wood Thrush populations have steadily declined in recent years, possibly because of habitat destruction on their wintering grounds in Central America. I would not be surprised if they are no longer heard in the small park where they brought me such joy.

The flutey song of the male is one of the most beautiful melodies of all our native birds. Upon hearing the musical, bell-like notes, Arthur Cleveland Bent felt the song transformed the woods "into a cathedral where peace and serenity abide." Henry David Thoreau was also impressed, feeling that the male's performance "deepens the significance of all things seen in the light of his strain."

The Wood Thrush's song starts with soft guttural *tut* notes, followed by an exquisite flutelike ramble that usually ends with a high trill: *tut-tut, eee-o-lay-o-leeeeeee.* Each male has ten or more different song patterns in his repertoire. Biologists have discovered that when two neighboring males interact, they alternate songs, and each tends to respond to the other's melody by singing a pattern in its repertoire that is clearly different from the song just heard. Thus, two countersinging males produce a musically diverse performance—a melodic sequence of varied song types in which none is repeated twice in a row. The alternation is often so precise and musically pleasing that from a distance it sounds as if one bird is singing. If you have woodies in your neighborhood, listen for these splendid duels!

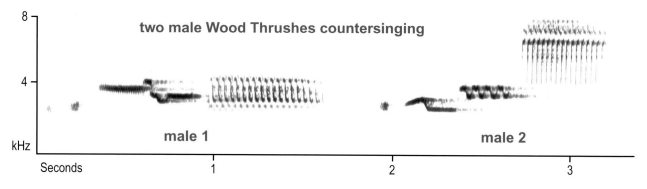

Hermit & Swainson's Thrushes

SPRING POND BOG is one of my favorite Adirondack recording locations. Owned by the Nature Conservancy, the preserve contains excellent examples of northern peatland bog and fen habitats. The bogland soundscape is uplifting, graced by the songs of White-throated Sparrow, Lincoln's Sparrow, Yellow-bellied Flycatcher, Nashville Warbler, and a variety of other northern birds, including the beautiful flutelike songs of Hermit Thrush and Swainson's Thrush.

During my first visit to the preserve, I arrived before dawn and placed my stereo microphone at the edge of a small quaking bog, nestled among some conifers. At first light, the dawn chorus began to unfold, and a Hermit Thrush soon appeared, spinning his flutey songs from the top of a tamarack tree not far to my right. Moments later, to my delight, another Hermit Thrush landed in a spruce tree to my left, and he immediately began to alternate his songs with those of the first thrush, producing a pleasing counterpoint effect. I donned my headphones and listened ecstatically—my first example of two male Hermit Thrushes countersinging. Then it dawned on me that something was very wrong. "The second thrush," I thought, "is *not* a Hermit Thrush. It's a Swainson's Thrush! I can tell by the upward spiral pattern of its notes. Holy smoke, can I believe my ears? Two entirely different species alternating songs with almost perfect rhythm. How lucky I am to record this unusual behavior."

The two northern thrushes look much alike—pale brownish with spotted breasts. But the Hermit has a reddish tail. Their songs are flutey, but different. The Hermit begins each song with a pure tone followed by a jumble of flutey notes. The Swainson's song lacks the pure tone beginning and spirals upward in pitch. Listen to the recording I made at Spring Pond Bog. You will have no trouble telling the two species apart. And it will be completely evident that the two birds are indeed interacting. Their countersinging is not a chance event. I think this is very special indeed.

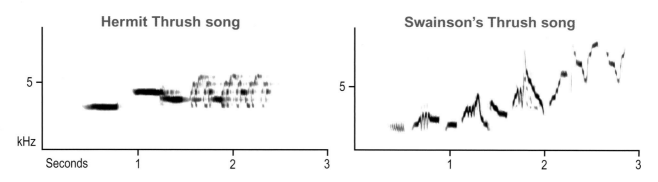

Swainson's Thrush

32

Thrush Flight Calls

ON A LATE MAY NIGHT in 1985, Bill Evans camped on a bluff overlooking the St. Croix River in southern Minnesota. While drifting to sleep, his attention was drawn outward to the faint sounds made by birds flying overhead in night migration. Bill tuned in to this music and lay awake for hours, enthralled by the beauty of the voices trickling down from the river of birds passing overhead. This single lucid experience catapulted Bill into his life's work. Now, more than twenty years later, he is a leading expert in the field and has coauthored *Flight Calls of Migratory Birds,* the first audio guide to the phenomenon. He has also designed inexpensive microphone and recording devices, which are available to anyone who wants to join in the research effort (see reference on page 124).

Many birds, especially songbirds, give calls during spring and fall migration, particularly during night flights, but also during the day. Night calling of many species peaks well after midnight, in the several hours preceding dawn. It takes considerable training to identify the plethora of notes that can be heard during peak migration periods. These days, biologists study night calling with the help of computers that analyze many hours of recordings and isolate significant calls, sometimes even identifying them to species. Still in its infancy, this specialized discipline is expanding rapidly.

To appreciate what is involved, consider the distinct flight calls of four native thrushes: the Hermit Thrush, Wood Thrush, Swainson's Thrush, and Veery. The Hermit's call is a loud *heeee,* the Wood's a buzzy *zeee,* the Swainson's a whistled *whee,* and the Veery's a variable *vee-yer* or *vee-yee.* I'm sure you will hear the differences. So why not tune in to this amazing migration spectacle next spring or fall? Choose a night when the sky is clear and the wind is light. Go to a high spot in the countryside in the wee hours before dawn and listen for subtle avian voices overhead. With luck, you will soon be completely absorbed in this great marvel enacted under the cover of night.

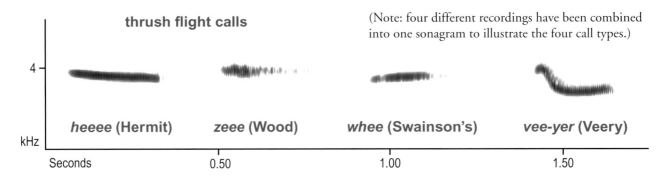

thrush flight calls

(Note: four different recordings have been combined into one sonagram to illustrate the four call types.)

4 —

heeee (Hermit)   *zeee* (Wood)   *whee* (Swainson's)   *vee-yer* (Veery)

kHz

Seconds   0.50   1.00   1.50

Hermit Thrush

Wood Thrush

Veery

Swainson's Thrush

33

Northern Mockingbird

MIMUS POLYGLOTTOS means "many-tongued mimic" and is a well-chosen scientific name for a bird that most folks immediately recognize—the Northern Mockingbird, named for its habit of imitating the sounds of other species. John Burroughs referred to the mocker as "*Our* nightingale" because his prominent musical song is often heard at night. Interestingly, there is a famous story about several European Nightingales that were imported and kept in cages near Lake Wales, Florida. As predicted, the nightingales were soon singing, but to everyone's surprise, the local mockingbirds quickly took to imitating their melodies. Before long, nightingale strains could be heard throughout the land of orange groves, as resident mockers enthusiastically sang their pleasing imitations.

Common and widespread, the mockingbird is found throughout the United States and is gradually expanding its range northward into Canada. A year-round resident of suburbs, farmland, and second-growth habitats, mockers frequent yards and gardens, where they aggressively swoop at dogs or cats that pass through their territories. Mockers sing mostly from February through August, but are occasionally heard in winter. Most singing occurs at dawn, although unmated males sing at night, especially during moonlit periods. Females may also sing, but their song is softer and less complex.

Male song bouts are composed of distinct song phrases, each repeated three or more times before switching to a new phrase. Many song phrases are faithful imitations of sounds made by other birds. I have many recordings of mockingbird song, but my all-time favorite is from the Tall Timbers Research Station near Tallahassee, Florida. I was recording a male when a Great-crested Flycatcher sounded off in the background, giving spirited *prrrrrrt* calls. The mocker paused as the flycatcher vocalized, as if listening, and then erupted with convincing *prrrrrrt* imitations. I could hardly believe my ears.

Northern Mockingbird imitation of Great-crested Flycatcher *prrrrrrt* call
(Note: two different recordings have been combined into one sonagram.)

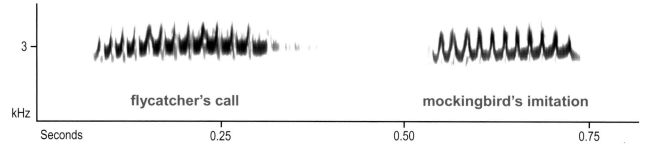

flycatcher's call   mockingbird's imitation

34

European Starling

DESPISED BY MANY, the European Starling is an introduced species that competes with native birds for nesting cavities, whether natural or manmade. A Eurasian species celebrated for their iridescent plumage and complex song, about sixty starlings were released in 1890 in New York City's Central Park as part of a misguided attempt to populate the city with the birds mentioned in Shakespeare's plays. The result was unexpected and devastating. Within 60 years, starlings reached the Pacific Coast. And now, 115 years later, they number more than two hundred million, spread over most of the continent. Starlings breed quickly, are very aggressive, and readily displace native species from their nests, often pecking open eggs and killing nestlings. They form huge noisy flocks that consume crops and spread diseases. The starling seems to be a veritable curse. Would that Shakespeare had never sung their praise! There is nothing good to say about a starling—or is there?

The starling is an exceptional vocalist, renowned for its ability to mimic the sounds of other birds and animals as well as inanimate sources. Aside from typical wheezy calls, alarm chatter, and distress screams, males produce songs of two types: short "whistled songs" and more complex "warbled songs." Whistled songs are fairly loud and consist of just two or three notes. In contrast, warbled songs are softer (at least in the beginning), but are extended performances that can last well over a minute. Usually beginning with clear whistles, warbled songs incorporate an improbable assortment of trills, rattles, chatters, sputters, and popping noises; the bird repeats most phrases a number of times and adds imitations along the way. Warbled songs seem to gradually build in volume and excitement, until the end, when the song suddenly loses steam and ends with drawn-out squeals. I was fortunate enough to capture a great recording of a warbled song by a starling that was nesting under the eaves of a friend's garage. I think you will agree that it is an amazing performance, quite deserving of poetic praise.

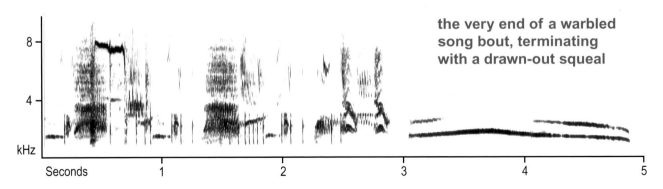

the very end of a warbled song bout, terminating with a drawn-out squeal

male singing

35

Black-throated Green Warbler

I WELL REMEMBER making my first recording of a Black-throated Green Warbler. I was walking along the bottom of a steep, wooded ravine in Shindagin Hollow, not far from my home in Ithaca, New York. From high in a hemlock tree came a faint buzzy refrain: *zeeee, zeeee, soo-soo, zee.* I grabbed my gear and scrambled up the slope in hot pursuit. Unfortunately (for me), the little bird flew quickly uphill. I ran full speed after him, parabolic mike in hand and heavy recorder dangling at my side. Completely exhausted, I finally overtook the songster on a high ridge. I got my recording, but alas, it proved useless because of my heavy breathing! I was disappointed, to be sure, but not long afterward I got great recordings of another male who sang repeatedly from a nearby perch. This scenario has unfolded time and again during my years of bird recording. I exhaust myself getting a lousy recording and then, when I least expect it, my quarry lands in front of me and sings as if he's been paid to please me.

The Black-throated Green Warbler inhabits mixed and coniferous forests and is common in the northeastern states, the upper Midwest, and in Canada from Newfoundland to Alberta. (The species also follows the Appalachian Mountain chain south into Georgia and Alabama.) Like many other wood warblers, male Black-throated Green Warblers have two song types. The leisurely one I described above, *zeeee, zeeee, soo-soo, zee,* is given primarily at dawn and dusk and during aggressive interactions between males. It is a unique and pleasant forest melody, a wheezy whispering sound of hemlock woods and northern boreal forests, often likened to the phrase *trees, trees, murmuring trees.* The other pattern is the more commonly heard daytime song, a spirited *see-see-see-see-soo-zee,* which functions to attract a female or maintain an existing pair bond. See if you can tell the two song types apart.

two song types of the Black-throated Green Warbler

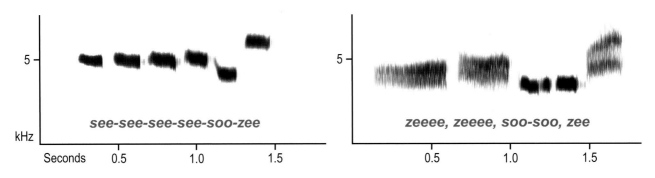

36

Ovenbird

ROBERT FROST, in his poem "The Oven Bird," was clearly impressed by the Ovenbird's ringing song: "There is a singer everyone has heard, / Loud, a mid-summer and a mid-wood bird, / Who makes the solid tree trunks sound again." We can only guess at what Frost really heard. He might be referring to the subtle echoes of songs off tree trunks, but more likely he is celebrating the echolike effect produced when one male sings and another male immediately answers, overlapping his song with the first.

The Ovenbird is a denizen of mature forests of the East, Northeast, upper Midwest, and Canada. The species is named for its habit of building a spherical, oven-shaped ground nest with a side entrance. A member of the warbler family, this common forest bird looks a lot like a thrush, with spotted underside and olive-brown back. Its primary song is a ringing series of whistled phrases that gradually build in loudness, sounding like *tea-cher, tea-cher, Tea-cher, Tea-cher, TEA-CHER, TEA-CHER*!

While the normal song is a delight to behold, it is a little boring in that males repeat their song time and again without variation. However, the Ovenbird makes up for this by performing an intricate "flight song," which is given at dusk and during moonlit nights. After most birds have retired for the night, the male Ovenbird gives several high-pitched chips and then suddenly rises into the air and flutters over the treetops, sending forth a complex series of high chips, warbles, and buzzes. John Burroughs described the performance as "an ecstasy of song . . . one of the rarest bits of bird melody to be heard." Thoreau was also moved, writing, "I hear the night warbler, breaking out as in his dreams." Because of its unpredictability, the flight song is exceedingly difficult to record. My attempts to capture the performance have all failed. The two examples on the disc are the result of dogged persistence by my pals Ted Mack and Wil Hershberger, both of whom deserve gold stars for their efforts!

Ovenbird flight song

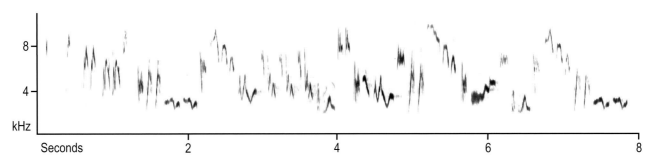

37

Summer Tanager

A TREETOP BIRD of the South, the brightly colored male Summer Tanager is difficult to spot because he is usually hidden behind leaves. Be persistent! He will eventually come into the open, and if direct sun illuminates his rosy red feathers, you'll get a glimpse that you'll remember forever (see cover photo). The species is common throughout the Southeast and ranging westward to California; its northern limit extends from Pennsylvania to Iowa. In much of the East, the Summer Tanager shares its range with the Scarlet Tanager (page 90), the latter being distinguished by jet-black wings and tail.

The song of the Summer Tanager is robinlike, but with a rough edge to its notes that gives it a noticeably burry quality. Songs typically last two to three seconds and are separated by about ten seconds of silence. Interestingly, the Summer Tanager has an alternate song that it sings at the break of dawn. It can go on for ten or more minutes and is composed of melodic whistled phrases given at a rate of about one or two per second. I first recorded Summer Tanager dawn song in Caledon Natural Area along the Potomac River in Virginia. It was too dark for me to see the male, who was singing from the top of an oak tree, and I actually thought I was recording an atypical American Robin. Subsequently, I had several bird experts listen to the recording, but everyone seemed confused about who the singer was. Finally, tanager expert Doug Robinson (author of a monograph on the species) verified that I had indeed recorded the dawn song of the Summer Tanager. It is not well known among birders, no doubt because one has to be on location at the crack of dawn in order to hear it.

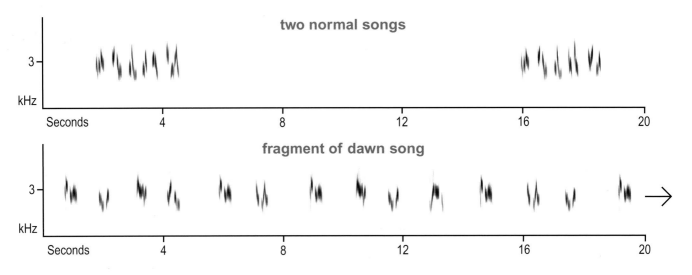

38

Scarlet Tanager

CAMPED BENEATH HEMLOCKS on a bluff overlooking a small creek near my home, I was awakened by the flutey songs of Hermit Thrushes that sprang from the valley like tinkling fairy music. Dawn had arrived, but I was not there to record thrushes. I slid from my sleeping bag and fumbled with my equipment, readying myself for my true quarry. Suddenly, a single *chick-bree* call fell from the canopy above. I aimed my microphone, and soon I had a smile on my face because I was capturing precisely what I'd come for: the dawn song of the Scarlet Tanager.

A vibrant red bird with black wings and tail, the male Scarlet Tanager is one of the most striking of our native songbirds (the female is dull yellow). He makes his home in the eastern deciduous forest biome, ranging from northern Georgia, Alabama, and Arkansas northward into Canada. Like his relative the Summer Tanager (page 88), he is a secretive bird of the treetops and is rarely seen, unless one follows the song and is lucky enough to catch a glimpse of the male in the dense canopy.

The Scarlet Tanager's distinctive call sounds like *chick-bree* or *chip-burr*. Typical songs are whistled and robinlike but have a noticeably hoarse or burry quality, described by Roger Tory Peterson as sounding like a robin with a sore throat: *queer, queery, queerit, queer.* Songs are brief, lasting two seconds or less, and separated by seven or eight seconds of silence. At dawn, however, the male sings a more spirited sequence. Whistled phrases still have the telltale burry quality, but there are no long pauses between phrases, and *chick-bree* calls may occur throughout. A dawn song bout may ramble on for many minutes before the male finally switches to his typical daytime pattern. Scarlet Tanager dawn song is not well known, and scientists to date seem to have overlooked it altogether, along with the analogous dawn song of the Summer Tanager. I hope you appreciate the example on the disc, which I captured that memorable morning in the hemlock grove overlooking the creek.

fragment of dawn song (with *chick-bree* call at beginning)

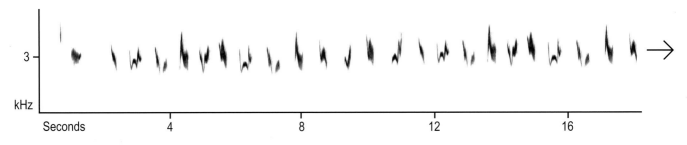

39

Northern Cardinal

FAMILIAR TO ALL, the Northern Cardinal is named for the male's bright red plumage, the same color as the long red gowns traditionally worn by cardinals of the Catholic faith. Formerly a bird of the South, the cardinal has expanded its range throughout the East and is now found as far north as Ontario and Quebec. Cardinals also range westward to the Great Plains and the desert regions of Arizona.

Cardinals are resident year-round, and pairs often remain together from year to year. Loose flocks form in fall and winter but disband as males begin singing and courting in late winter, when the male's bright whistles can be heard even while snow is still on the ground. The cardinal has a rich and pleasing song composed of loud, rapidly repeated whistles. Most songs are two-parted, with common patterns sounding like *purdy, purdy, purdy, wheet-wheet-wheet-wheet,* or *what-cheer, what-cheer, whoit-whoit-whoit-whoit,* or even a simple *whit-whit-whit-whit-whit.* Each male has about eight to ten different song types in his repertoire, and neighboring males usually share a number of patterns. Males often sing back and forth, a phenomenon called countersinging, when forming territories in the spring or during interactions throughout the breeding season. Song-matching is also common, and sometimes two or three males in the same vicinity can be heard singing exactly the same song type, and then all switching to a new pattern after one male makes the change.

As if to complicate matters, female cardinals also sing. What's more, they often countersing and match song types with their mate. So the next time you hear two cardinals singing back and forth, don't assume that it's two males interacting—go find the birds and verify just who is doing the talking. On the compact disc, you will hear a great example of song-matching among neighboring males, along with a superb recording of a female alternating songs with her mate, provided by Greg Budney, curator of the Macaulay Library at the Cornell Laboratory of Ornithology.

mates countersinging and song-matching

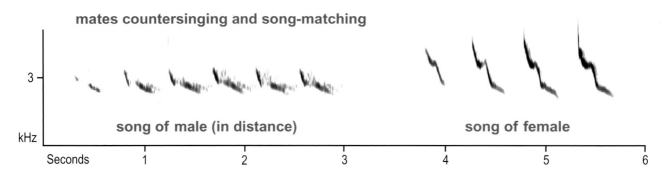

song of male (in distance)   song of female

40

Rose-breasted Grosbeak

HIGH IN A TREE, rose breast shining brightly in the sun, a black-and-white bird commenced to sing its rollicking melody—rich robinlike whistles, but prettier than a robin, with notes more rounded and appealing to the human ear. What a satisfying experience, seeing and hearing a Rose-breasted Grosbeak in full song as I canoed in an Adirondack marsh in early June.

Resembling the song of the American Robin, the grosbeak's composition is fuller in tone and more melodic in effect, often likened to that of "a robin who has taken music lessons." Males have a variety of different song types, and some songs end with delightfully musical flourishes. Each song, composed of a series of discrete warbled phrases, lasts about six seconds, and there are usually six seconds or more of silence between songs. Songs may also be accompanied by *chink* notes, the diagnostic call of the species. Female rose-breasteds also sing, but I've never managed to record one. Their song has not been described in detail, but it is thought to occur mostly around the nest.

The Rose-breasted Grosbeak occasionally sings a different song—I call it "extended song"—a long ramble of phrases that can last a minute or more. Scientists think this is a courtship song, given by males during the pairing phase. Whatever its purpose, the grosbeak's extended song is truly a jewel of spring, but a performance that is rarely heard, even by avid listeners. Listen for it when the grosbeaks return from migration and the woods come alive with their sweet melodies.

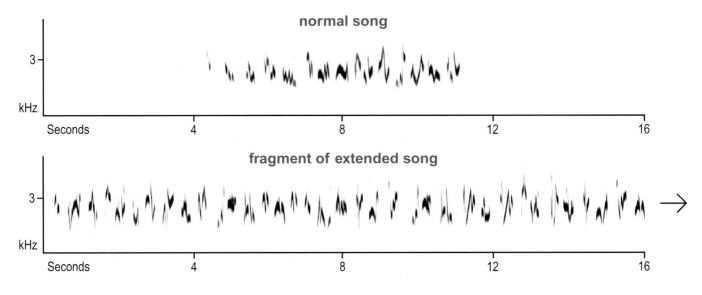

41

Grasshopper Sparrow

WHEN I WAS YOUNG I thought the word "sparrow" referred to one particular bird. Little did I know that North America is home to more than thirty different kinds of sparrows that live in a wide range of habitats, from dense forest to open grassy areas. Most are drab brown, but some have reddish feathers, white throats or crowns, and other obvious patches of color. Some have beautiful songs, but a number have songs that are unmusical, high-pitched, and insectlike.

One of my favorites is the Grasshopper Sparrow, named because its diminutive song sounds like the lispy call of a grasshopper: *tip, tup, zeeeee.* This species inhabits grassy meadows across much of North America, but it is easily overlooked. I experienced my first Grasshopper Sparrow in a meadow among the rolling hills of the Finger Lakes region of upstate New York. I was having a picnic with a friend when a male landed on a grass stem only twenty feet away and serenaded us with his buzzy song.

Surprisingly, males occasionally sing a remarkable "sustained song," an extremely rapid outburst of exceedingly high notes, quite unlike normal song (wait until you hear it slowed down to one-quarter speed, at which you can appreciate the complexity). Scientists are not sure what this special performance is all about, though they speculate it has something to do with attracting mates or maintaining pair bond. Whatever the meaning, the mere existence of two radically different song types captures my attention and draws me to this unassuming little musician of grasslands and meadows.

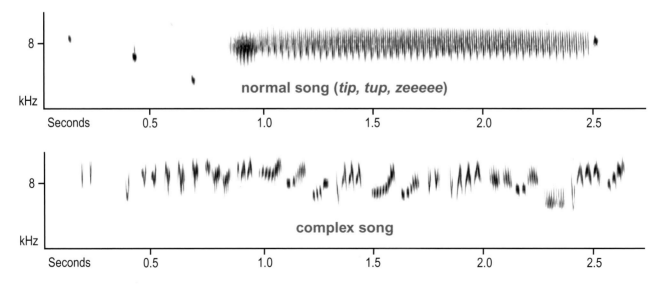

normal song (*tip, tup, zeeeee*)

complex song

42

Henslow's Sparrow

I MET MY FIRST Henslow's Sparrow while exploring a hilltop meadow. I kept hearing what I first thought was a cricket chirp—an extremely high-pitched, metallic *tsi-de-lick* coming from thick grass in front of me. I searched in vain for the source, which seemed to move each time I approached. Then, just when I was ready to give up, a small mouselike bird flitted to the top of a weed stalk, threw up its head, and sang its tiny squeak of a song before dropping back into the grass. You call that a bird song?

The Henslow's Sparrow, an inconspicuous little brown bird inhabiting grassy meadows in the Midwest and portions of the East, was named by John James Audubon in honor of John Stevens Henslow, a British professor of botany who subscribed to Audubon's early works. Surprisingly, Dr. Henslow never visited North America and never heard the sparrow's simple song. Roger Tory Peterson described the song as "one of the poorest vocal efforts of any bird." Personally, I think it's a grand effort and applaud the bird for practicing the law of parsimony—the judicious exercise of economy and frugality. The humble Henslow's Sparrow accomplishes his goal with the least amount of fuss. By singing less, he impresses me more! Of course, one should realize that my interpretation is clouded by the limitations of my human hearing. If I slow a song down using my computer, this "poor excuse" for a song transforms into a delightful musical cascade. Would that we could hear as the birds do!

To spice things up on the compact disc, I include a song I recently recorded in the middle of the night at Prairie State Park in southwestern Missouri. Yes, Henslow's Sparrows often sing at night. And this particular bird has a rather complex song that takes on new meaning when slowed to one-quarter speed. I'm confident that it will penetrate your heart and inflame your passion, like an arrow straight from Cupid's bow!

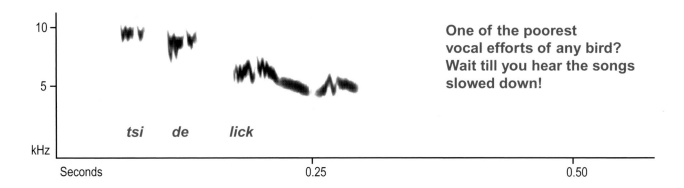

One of the poorest
vocal efforts of any bird?
Wait till you hear the songs
slowed down!

43

White-crowned Sparrow

I OBSERVED MY FIRST White-crowned Sparrow, a common migrant in upstate New York, at a bird feeder near my home. Although migrating males often sing, I was never able to capture one on tape until I traveled to Alaska, where this species is abundant. There I got superb recordings and photographs, and I also became aware of regional differences in song patterns.

White-crowned Sparrow song has been the subject of extensive research. Ornithologist Luis Baptista devoted much of his professional life to the species, documenting the fine structure of singing behavior and the roles of genetics and social interaction in song development. To the delight of his students, he also had the uncanny ability to whistle exact imitations of songs, albeit delivered at "half speed" and with a funny look on his face. Baptista observed that males in any particular area all share the same song type, while birds from other areas nearby sing noticeably different types. These different regional song patterns are termed "dialects" and indicate distinct breeding populations, which is very significant to those who study the evolution of birds. Apparently, young males learn their dialect shortly after they're born, by listening to adult males singing in their immediate surroundings.

In spite of the numerous dialects, a White-crowned's song is usually easy to recognize: one or more clear whistled tones followed by a series of buzzes, trills, or chips. If you're lucky enough to live where White-crowned Sparrows breed, tune in to their songs and learn your local dialect. Then, some gentle dawn, go for a long bike ride and listen to each male sing as you pass through his territory. Songs should all sound the same, until suddenly, without warning, you hear a distinct change as you pass from one dialect to the next. You may be surprised at how different the new pattern sounds.

White-crowned Sparrow song dialects

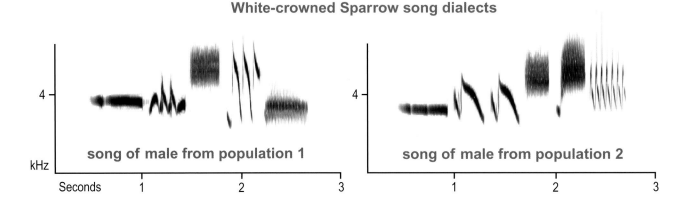

song of male from population 1

song of male from population 2

44

Bobolink

"A BUBBLING DELIRIUM of ecstatic music that flows from the gifted throat of the bird like sparkling champagne." What an apt poetic description of Bobolink song from the pen of the ornithologist Arthur Cleveland Bent. The exuberant notes produced by the male seem otherworldly in quality and, to my mind, resemble the silly sounds produced by R2-D2 in the *Star Wars* movies. The common name "Bobolink" actually refers to the song and is derived from the poem "Robert of Lincoln" by William Cullen Bryant, which describes the bird's breeding cycle and makes repeated reference to song. Here is the first stanza: "Merrily swinging on brier and weed, / Near to the nest of his little dame, / Over the mountain-side or mead, / Robert of Lincoln is telling his name: / Bob-o'-link, bob-o'-link, / Spink, spank, spink." Thank you, William, for giving birth to Bobolink!

The Bobolink frequents grassy meadows of the northern states and adjacent Canada. Also referred to as "skunk blackbird," the male has striking black-and-white plumage, making identification easy. Females are a buffy yellow-brown. Wintering in South America, Bobolinks migrate more than five thousand miles to and from their breeding grounds. Arriving at northern meadows in May, males stake out territories and court females by chasing them about in the air and singing ecstatically while perched or in flight.

Each male has a repertoire of two different songs, which are presented more or less randomly during a singing bout. Flight song, given as a male circles above his territory, is an extended performance in which two or more songs are strung together. Bobolink song is so amazing that it is impossible to describe with words. Only poetic references come close to capturing the essence. My favorite is by F. Schuyler Mathews, author of the classic *Field Book of Wild Birds and Their Music*. He refers to song as "a mad, reckless song-fantasia, an outbreak of pent-up irrepressible glee." Listen to the songs on the disc and maybe you too will be inspired to wax poetic about the Bobolink's ecstatic melody.

"a mad, reckless song-fantasia"

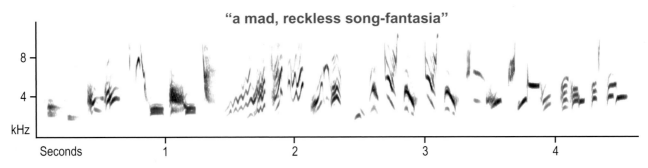

45

Brown-headed Cowbird

WHEN I BEGAN WORK on my book *Music of the Birds* (1999), I set about gathering photographs of singing birds. One of my first subjects was the Yellow Warbler. I found a male on territory among alder shrubs at the edge of a marsh. Before long, his mate appeared and led me directly to their nest. To my complete surprise, the nest was "double-tiered." In other words, the warblers had built a nest on top of a nest! Reading up on the subject, I discovered the reason. The nest had fallen victim to a female Brown-headed Cowbird, who had replaced the warbler eggs with her own. Most songbirds don't detect such an intrusion and raise cowbird young to adulthood, but the yellow warbler often responds adaptively, building a new nest over the top of the old one and laying a new clutch of eggs.

Brown-headed Cowbirds are brood parasites. They do not build nests of their own, but rather lay their eggs in the nests of other species, confident that the hosts will raise the young. Obviously, cowbirds harm the species they parasitize. Although their range has expanded greatly in the last two hundred years because of habitat disturbance by humans, cowbirds were originally prairie birds. Referred to as "buffalo birds," they followed buffalo and fed on insects associated with the herds.

Although cowbirds do not defend nesting territories, the male does have a song, given as he bows forward, cocks his wings, and spreads his tail. It is a thin high-pitched whistle, preceded by soft gurgling notes: *bublo-com-seeeee* or *glug-glug-gleeee*. In the spring, males gather in treetops, bowing and calling to one another or to females. Once paired, the female actually duets with her mate, giving a liquid chatter in obvious response to the male's display, often overlapping or even preceding his song. If you're walking down the sidewalk on a warm spring day and hear a "whistle-and-chatter duet," scan your surroundings until you find them—a male cowbird bowing and whistling to his lovely mate.

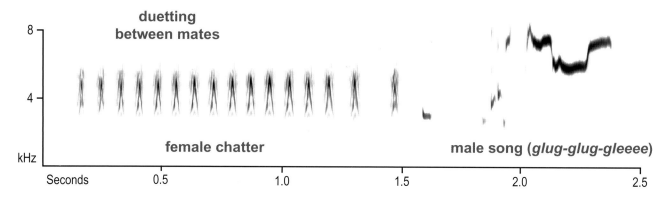

female

46

Red-winged Blackbird

EVEN CASUAL OBSERVERS of birds are familiar with Red-winged Blackbirds. Easily recognized by their black bodies and bright red shoulder patches, or "epaulets," migrating males arrive in flocks in late winter, drawing our attention with raucous calls and songs. Less obvious are the brownish females, which show up not long after the males and initiate the courtship phase. I remember when I spied my first female, perched on a cattail in a Missouri marsh. I had no idea it was a redwing until a male suddenly arrived on the scene and attempted copulation. Mystery solved!

Redwings nest in marshes and upland grassy habitats throughout most of North America. Males rigorously defend territories by singing from tall grass or cattails, or from shrubs and trees in their nesting areas. They also sing in flight. At the height of the breeding season, males accompany their songs with a "song-spread display," in which a male bows forward, opens his wings, and puffs out his epaulets as he sings. During nesting season, redwings often leave their nesting areas and travel in flocks to feed in farm fields, suburban and urban parks, or wherever else they can find food.

The song of the male, a vibrant *oak-a-leee* or *conk-la-reee,* is composed of two bright introductory notes followed by a terminal buzz or trill, although some songs include an additional note at the end: *conk-la-reee-ink.* Males have five or more different song types in their repertoires, but usually sing one type for long periods before switching to another. Calls include a sharp *chack,* various metallic notes and chips, and a loud penetrating *seee* or *see-yeer* given by males when alarmed near the nest.

Although many males are monogamous, having just one mate, some are polygynous and possess territories containing two or more females. Females defend small territories by chasing other females from the area around their nest and by giving a sputtery chatter that is referred to as "female song." What's more, a female often duets with her mate by delivering her sputter in response to his song.

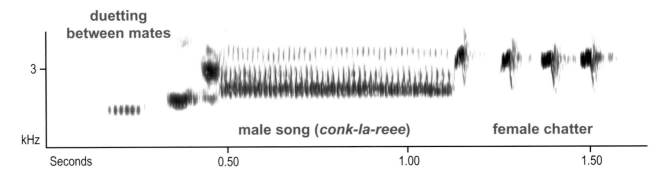

duetting between mates | male song (*conk-la-reee*) | female chatter

3 kHz · Seconds · 0.50 · 1.00 · 1.50

female giving chatter-song

47

Eastern & Western Meadowlarks

BORN IN MEXICO, MISSOURI, I grew up in farm country, with the sweet songs of meadowlarks gracing fields and meadows all around me. *Seee-yee-see-yeer* or *spring-o-the-year,* the males whistled from fence posts, telephone wires, and small trees, identifying themselves as Eastern Meadowlarks, though the western species could be found breeding less than fifty miles to the north.

Virtually identical in appearance, Eastern and Western Meadowlarks are best distinguished by voice, especially in the area of overlap running from Texas north to the upper Midwest and adjacent Canada. The song of the Eastern is composed of plaintive, slurred whistles, dropping in pitch at the end, and sometimes having a shrill or wavering quality. In contrast, the Western's song is a rich mixture of loud melodious notes, beginning with short whistles that are followed by variable gurgling phrases. The two species rarely interbreed, and studies have shown that hybrids are mostly sterile. Nonetheless, they live in the same habitats, and males defend their territories from intrusion by other males of both species, an unusual behavior that scientists refer to as "interspecific territoriality."

Interestingly, both species also have special extended flight songs that are rarely heard and very difficult to record. The Eastern Meadowlark's performance begins with several harsh calls given from a perch, followed by an ecstatic outburst of unmusical notes given on the wing, and lasting ten seconds or longer before the singer returns to his perch. To my knowledge, no recordings exist of the Eastern's flight song. In contrast, the Western's flight song begins with musical whistles that gradually speed up, at which time the male launches into a slow fluttering flight accompanied by his own ecstatic outburst of notes before returning to a perch. Luckily, my good friend and fellow recordist Ted Mack coincidentally captured a Western's flight song while he was recording prairie-chickens in southeastern Colorado. Ted's splendid recording is featured on the compact disc.

Western Meadowlark flight song (preceded by clear whistled notes)

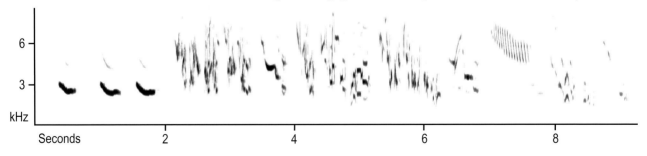

Western Meadowlark

48

Baltimore Oriole

NATURALIST MARK CATESBY described the Baltimore Oriole in 1731 in his seminal *Natural History of Carolina, Florida, and the Bahama Islands.* He called it "Baltimore Bird," explaining that orange and black were the colors of the Baltimores, a ruling family in the Maryland colony. Long referred to as Baltimore Oriole, the common name was changed to Northern Oriole in the late 1960s to combine it with the western Bullock's Oriole, then thought to be the same species. But further studies indicated that the two really are different species, so scientists recently changed the name back to Baltimore Oriole and once again gave species status to Bullock's Oriole.

The song of a male is a series of melodious whistled phrases that often can be easily imitated by a human whistler. Females occasionally sing, sometimes from the nest, but their songs are usually simpler than those of males. Males generally have one primary song pattern, but sing a number of variations by adding, subtracting, or rearranging certain phrases. Also, most males in a particular neighborhood have unique song patterns, allowing humans to recognize individuals, even from year to year as they migrate each spring to the same territory. This is not always the case, however. In his classic study of a small population, ornithologist David Beletsky discovered that about 70 percent of the males had unique song patterns, while 30 percent sang patterns that were nearly identical to those of neighboring males.

The primary call of the oriole is a grating chatter, given during aggressive encounters with other orioles and when humans or predators pass close to the nest. Another common call is a nasal *jeet-jeet-jeet,* apparently given during encounters between males. But my all-time favorite oriole call is the unique nasal begging call of the young, given by older nestlings and by fledglings for a week or two after leaving the nest: *dee-dee . . . dee-dee-dee-dee . . . dee-dee-dee.* If you have Baltimore Orioles in your neighborhood, listen for these telltale begging calls in midsummer when young are fledged. If you're lucky, you'll spot a youngster perched on a limb, crying out for food and being fed by one of its parents.

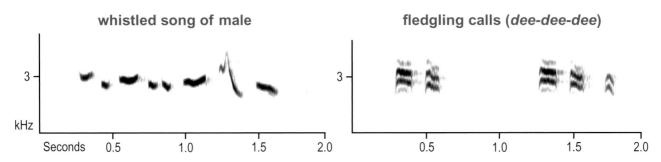

whistled song of male   fledgling calls (*dee-dee-dee*)

fledgling giving begging calls

49

American Goldfinch

JOHN BURROUGHS was moved by the singing behavior of male goldfinches in the spring. He observed that "all the goldfinches of a neighborhood collect together and hold a sort of musical festival . . . To the number of many dozens, they may be seen in some large tree, all singing and calling in the most joyous and vivacious manner . . . there is no sign of quarreling or fighting."

To be sure, goldfinches are social creatures, and they travel about in noisy flocks for most of the year. Only during the midsummer breeding period do males and females finally pair up to defend territories. Goldfinches range throughout the United States and southern Canada. They prefer open areas with scattered trees and may be seen in orchards, along roadsides, in yards and gardens, and among fields and meadows. The male in breeding plumage is brilliant yellow with black cap, wings, and tail. Females, immatures, and wintering males are dull in comparison. Breeding occurs quite late in the season, in mid-July, well after most other songbirds have nested.

Goldfinch song is high-pitched and sprightly. In spring, males sing long versions that ramble on for several minutes. Later in the summer, males sing in flight while courting females. Once territories are established, males give short versions of songs. Goldfinches are also known for their sweet *perchickory* flight call, given during their trademark "undulating flight," in which the calls are coordinated with rhythmic swoops. The contact call of the species is a vibrant *soo-eet* and the alarm call is a repeated *beer-bee.* But of all the goldfinch calls, the most interesting for me is the sharp, insistent *chip-pee, chip-pee* given by young for several weeks after they leave the nest—it reminds me of the calls of Spring Peepers. Listen for it in late summer, when goldfinch families gather in hedgerows and brushy patches, the young begging excitedly for food.

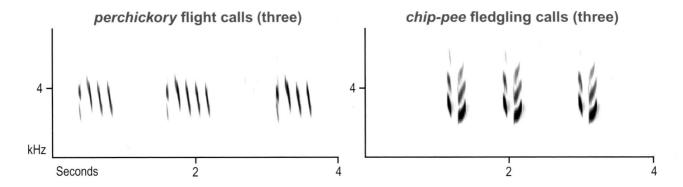

perchickory **flight calls (three)**   *chip-pee* **fledgling calls (three)**

50

House Finch

ORIGINALLY A WESTERN BIRD, the House Finch was introduced to Long Island in 1940 and rapidly spread throughout the East, aggressively pushing westward to close the gap between the two populations. Over most of its range, the male has a bright red head and breast. In certain populations, however, male color ranges from orange to pale yellow or colorless, because of the lack of carotenoid pigments in their food. House Finches are common feeder birds, familiar to almost everyone.

The song of the male is a rapid musical warble, lasting about three seconds. Song patterns are highly variable among individuals, although local dialects have been identified in some areas of the East. Songs no doubt attract mates, but they may not signify territoriality because males sometimes sing in close proximity to one another without showing any aggression. Females occasionally sing a simplified song, though its function is unknown. Males also perform a striking "butterfly flight" in which they flutter slowly to a height of nearly one hundred feet and then glide back to their perch, singing continuously. Occurring early in the season, butterfly flight is probably related to pair formation.

A rarer song type is the pre-copulation song of the male, given only in the presence of a receptive female. One spring dawn, I approached a male who was singing excitedly in a tree in my hometown of Ithaca, New York. With head cocked, he was flitting from perch to perch around his mate, singing continuously, with lots of high-pitched notes thrown in. The female assumed a crouched posture and vibrated her wings as he sang. She appeared to be soliciting copulation—and you might guess what happened next! Actually, they didn't copulate (oh darn), most likely because of my presence, but the House Finch expert Geoff Hill assures me that copulation was undoubtedly the prime intention. Listen for yourself, and see if you can sense the erotic impulse overwhelming the mind of the singer.

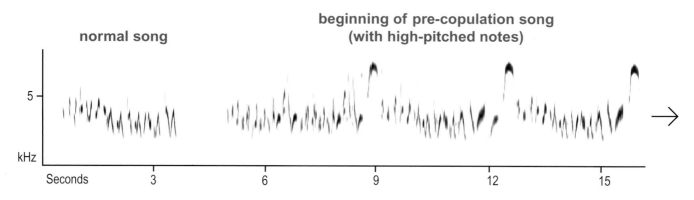

normal song

beginning of pre-copulation song
(with high-pitched notes)

All About Bird Sounds

This section is borrowed from pages 17–22 of *Common Birds and Their Songs*
by Lang Elliott and Marie Read (Houghton Mifflin, 1998)

Birds communicate in many ways, and sound is one of the most important. Luckily, humans can eavesdrop on this bird conversation—songs and calls not only inform us of the presence of birds in our surroundings, they allow us to identify species and alert us to interesting behavior.

Bird sounds are perhaps best understood according to their functions. Consider the difference between what we term a *song* and a *call.* In the simplest sense, song is a loud, complex, and often musical utterance used mostly by male birds to establish and maintain a breeding territory. Calls, in contrast, are simpler and usually softer sounds used by both sexes to communicate alarm, hunger, aggression, and a variety of other motivational states.

Until recently, the word "song" was used primarily to describe the musical utterances produced by *songbirds,* a group famous for its members' voices (familiar songbirds include the wrens, sparrows, finches, orioles, tanagers, and warblers). However, a functional definition argues that song occurs in many other bird groups as well, including shorebirds, game birds, owls, doves, and woodpeckers. From this perspective, the musical cooing of a male Mourning Dove is functionally equivalent to the lively song of a male American Robin.

To humans, a singing performance may appear spontaneous—males perch in trees and shrubs, or fly overhead, exuberantly repeating song after song for no obvious reason. Because song is often beautiful and seemingly unprompted, we are tempted to explain its motivation in human terms: perhaps song is an expression of the joy of life. Actually, song is a display. A singing male is communicating territory ownership—warning neighboring males of the same species that his territory is occupied and will be defended. While song is usually produced only by males, females of a variety of species are known to sing, although their songs are often weaker and less complex than the male's version. Singing may also advertise availability, helping unpaired males attract potential mates. And once the birds have mated, song may help maintain their pair bond.

We usually consider songs to be *vocal* sounds, produced by special organs in a bird's throat. However, certain *nonvocal* sounds can be construed as songs. Consider, for instance, the drumming of woodpeckers (produced by rapping the beak against wood) or the drumming of the grouse (produced by beating the wings). Both these signals are used during the breeding season to attract mates and define territories, and hence might be loosely classified as bird songs.

Black-throated Green Warbler

Calls, in contrast to songs, are often simple, brief sounds, like the cardinal's metallic *chip* or the robin's sharp *peek.* Many calls are subtle, being audible only at close range, and likely to be missed by the casual observer. Nonetheless, calls can be very informative. When studied in detail, most bird species are found to have a variety of different calls in their sound repertoires. Each call is usually given in a specific context or in response to a specific situation, alerting us to behavior in progress. Being able to recognize, identify, and interpret calls can tell us if aggression or courtship is occurring, if a bird is alarmed at the presence of a predator, or if a fledgling is being fed by its parents. Truly, understanding the meanings of bird calls provides us with our most intimate glimpses into birds' lives.

In this book we use the term "song" to refer to complex territorial vocalizations given mostly by males during the breeding season. Other vocalizations are referred to as "calls," and we include their functions when known. In addition, *nonvocal* sounds are described when they play a major role in the life of a bird.

Sound Repertoires

All the auditory signals produced by a given species make up its *sound repertoire.* Some birds produce only a few sounds, while others have a greater variety of calls and song types. Scientific studies suggest that most birds use at least a dozen different vocal displays to communicate with one another. Many of these sounds are subtle and used only at close range, during intimate communication.

Looking at song in particular, we discover that some birds, such as the Indigo Bunting and Common Yellowthroat, have one song type they repeat over and over with little variation. At the other extreme, species such as the Northern Mockingbird and the Marsh Wren may produce hundreds of different song variations. Why are there such huge differences in song repertoire size? The answer to this question is unclear, and research on this topic is ongoing.

More About Bird Song

Certain songbirds imitate the sounds of other bird species, incorporating these sounds into their songs. The Northern Mockingbird and the European Starling are well-known examples. The starling even mimics mechanical sounds and the noises of animals other than birds. Catbirds and thrashers are also imitators, as are Blue Jays, which often mimic the calls of hawks. Among birders, the ability to recognize which species these birds are imitating is a prime test of knowledge of bird sound.

Territorial disputes between male songbirds may include an interesting vocal behavior known as *countersinging,* in which neighboring males of the same species engage in song duels, singing back and forth in an alternating fashion. Northern Cardinals, Tufted Titmice, and Wood Thrushes often duel with song. A related behavior is *song-matching,* in which participants in a countersinging bout match each other's song types. The Marsh Wren is famed for this behavior.

In some species, both members of a pair may sing together in a close-knit fashion. Such *song duetting* occurs primarily in tropical birds, but some temperate-zone species show related behavior. For instance, female Brown-headed Cowbirds and female Red-winged Blackbirds often give sputtering chatters as the male sings. Duetting may help reinforce pair bonds while also sending a strong territorial message to neighbors of the same species.

More About Bird Calls

Contact calls are used between mates or among members of a flock or family group to indicate the location of the caller. In gregarious species they function in group cohesion. Such calls are often given when a bird takes flight or lands, providing important information to other birds in the vicinity.

Many birds have calls that they give primarily in flight. Eastern Bluebirds, for instance, often give a melodic *turalee* call when flying. The commonly heard flight call of the American Goldfinch sounds like *perchikory*. Less well known are the subtle calls given during nocturnal migration flights—elusive chips and whistles made by invisible songbirds flying overhead in the dark of night.

Alarm calls are given in situations of danger and often serve to summon the mate. They are characteristically short and sharp and tend to sound rather similar across different species. In fact, many birds pay attention to the alarm calls of other species and respond with specific behaviors. The Black-capped Chickadee offers a good example: its high warning cries given when a hawk flies overhead frequently cause nuthatches and woodpeckers, associating with the chickadees in mixed winter flocks, to freeze in place or dive for cover.

Some calls have highly specialized functions or occur only under very specific circumstances. The Eastern Phoebe, for instance, has a unique *nest-site-showing call,* which it gives while fluttering in front of a potential nest site when its mate is nearby. And the female American Goldfinch has a distinct call that she uses to solicit feeding by her mate while she is incubating the eggs in their nest.

The *begging calls* of nestlings are often shrill, repetitive sounds, which accelerate as the parent bird approaches the nest with food. After the fledglings leave the nest, their typical behavior is to crouch and vibrate their wings, all the while giving excited calls to elicit feeding.

More About Nonvocal Sounds

Nonvocal sounds used in communication are commonplace among birds. Woodpeckers rap their bills on resonant wood to produce drumming sounds that have territorial and courtship functions. Herons and owls clatter or snap their bills during aggressive or alarm situations. A male Ruffed Grouse attracts females by perching on a log and rapidly beating its wings to produce a thumping sound. Pigeons, doves, woodcock, snipe, and hummingbirds make whistling or buzzing sounds with their wings during flight and incorporate these sounds into their courtship and other displays. In fact, the more we study a bird the more likely we are to discover subtle nonvocal sounds, such as bill clicking, tapping, or feather ruffling, that are used as displays during intimate social interactions. The study of a bird's communication system is not complete until its nonvocal sounds have been investigated.

Baltimore Oriole

Acknowledgments

Many people have contributed to the creation of this book, and I offer sincere thanks to all my friends for their unwavering support. I am particularly indebted to Ted Mack, my longtime nature pal, who has accompanied me on many field expeditions through the years. Ted's recordings are featured numerous times on the compact disc. Without his help, this book would not have happened. Wil Hershberger has also been a faithful friend. We have recorded and photographed together and discussed ideas of all sorts. Wil's splendid photos grace many pages in this book. Thanks also to Catherine Landis, Monica Plisch, and John Cancalosi, who offered unfailing personal support throughout the process. And I cannot fail to mention my comrades at the Finger Lakes Land Trust, where my sound studio is located. They provided me with a stimulating social milieu as I slaved away in front of my computer for months on end.

Special thanks also goes to Don Kroodsma for reading my essays and alerting me to incorrect or misleading statements. I am deeply indebted to Don and a host of other bird-song biologists — their field research has shed light on the singing life of birds, giving me direction and focus and providing me with the substance of many of my essays. Without them, I would have far less to celebrate. I have also benefited from the excellent editing of Dan Otis, who lives just down the street, and Lisa White of Houghton Mifflin. Anne Chalmers, also of Houghton Mifflin, provided invaluable help with the overall design of the book. I also want to thank all the photographers who have contributed to this book, especially Marie Read, Brian Small, Wil Hershberger, Steve and Dave Maslowski, and Robert Royse. Their photos are so stunning that many people will buy this book just for the pictures.

Last but not least, I applaud the bird musicians themselves, who have given me the opportunity to celebrate the beauty of their songs. Thank you, beautiful birds, for filling my life with your melodies.

Wood Thrush

Sources and Further Reading

Books About Bird Song

The following four books provide considerable insight into the science and poetry of bird song. They take four different approaches, and I recommend them all.

Donald Kroodsma. 2005. *The Singing Life of Birds: The Art and Science of Listening to Birdsong* (book and compact disc). Boston: Houghton Mifflin Company. A compelling, personal account by Don of his many years of fieldwork studying bird song.

David Rothenberg. 2005. *Why Birds Sing: A Journey Through the Mystery of Bird Song.* New York: Basic Books. A unique and revealing treatise on bird song by a philosophy professor who is also a jazz composer and musician.

Peter Marler and Hans Slabbekoorn (editors). 2004. *Nature's Music: The Science of Birdsong* (book and compact disc). San Diego: Elsevier Academic Press. An up-to-date technical summary of the science of bird song, including chapters by eighteen different biologists.

Lang Elliott. 1999. *Music of the Birds: A Celebration of Bird Song* (book and compact disc). Boston: Houghton Mifflin Company. Chock-full of quotations from early poets and naturalists, this book focuses on the appreciation of bird song, and includes more than one hundred photos of singing birds.

NOTE: To learn about other books and compact discs by Lang Elliott, go to: www.songsofwildbirds.com.

BNA Online

An excellent reference summarizing our current scientific knowledge about native birds is The Birds of North America Online (BNA Online), an affordable subscription-based service offered by the Cornell University Laboratory of Ornithology and the American Ornithologists' Union. Accessed via the Internet, the BNA species monographs are updated as new studies appear and include detailed descriptions of the sound repertoires of each species. In addition, actual sound recordings of songs and calls of each species are being added as they become available. I highly recommend BNA Online to anyone who is serious about the study and appreciation of bird song. To view demonstration monographs and learn more about subscribing, go to: bna.birds.cornell.edu/BNA/.

Sources of Quotes and Other Information Presented in Essays

While drawing heavily on my personal experiences to write the essays, I also relied on BNA Online as my primary source of scientific information. A number of additional sources are listed below, including references to quotes and to specific scientific studies.

Common Loon
- McIntyre, J. W. 1988. *The Common Loon: Spirit of Northern Lakes.* Minneapolis: University of Minnesota Press.

American Bittern
- Andersen, Hans Christian. *The Marsh King's Daughter.* First published in 1858.

Bald Eagle & Red-tailed Hawk
- Bent quote from: Bent, A. C. 1937. Life histories of North American birds of prey. *U.S. National Museum Bulletin* 167: 331.
- Brewster quote from: Brewster, W. 1925. The birds of the Lake Umbagog region of Maine. *Bulletin of the Museum of Comparative Zoology* 66:211–402.
- Benjamin Franklin quote from a letter he wrote to his daughter, Sarah Bache, dated January 26, 1784. In Franklin, Benjamin. 1905. *The Writings of Benjamin Franklin,* vol. 10. Edited by Albert Henry Smyth. New York: The Macmillan Company.

Wild Turkey
- Benjamin Franklin reference: Franklin, *Writings,* vol. 10.

Sandhill Crane
- To learn more about Sadako Sasaki, go to: www.naturesound.com/sadako.html.
- Learn more about cranes at the International Crane Foundation Web site: www.savingcranes.org.

American Woodcock
- Leopold, Aldo. 1949. *A Sand County Almanac.* New York. Oxford University Press.

Common Snipe
- Thoreau quote from: Thoreau, Henry David. 1899. *Walden, or, Life in the Woods.* New York: T. Y. Crowell and Company. Page 333.

Atlantic Puffin
- For information about the restoration work of Dr. Stephen Kress, go to the Project Puffin Web site: www.projectpuffin.org.

Great Horned Owl
- The Passamaquoddy legend can be found at www.firstpeople.us/FP-Html-Legends/TheOwlHusband-Passamaquoddy.html.
- Bourke, John G. 1886. *An Apache Campaign in the Sierra Madre.* New York: Scribners.

Barred Owl
- The Cherokee legend can be found at www.cherokee.org/Culture/LiteraturePage.asp?ID-22.
- Kroodsma, Donald. 2005. *The Singing Life of Birds.* Boston: Houghton Mifflin Company. Pages 336–46.

Eastern Screech-Owl
- Ritchison, G., P. M. Cavanagh, J. R. Belthoff, and E. J. Sparks. 1988. The singing behavior of eastern screech-owls: Seasonal timing and response to playback of conspecfic song. *Condor* 90:648–52

Whip-poor-will & Chuck-will's-widow
- Halle quote from: Halle, Louis J. 1947. *Spring in Washington*. New York: William Sloane Associates. Page 131.

Pileated & Ivory-billed Woodpeckers
- For information on the rediscovery of the Ivory-billed Woodpecker, go to: www.birds.cornell.edu.

Eastern Wood-Pewee
- Craig, W. 1926. The twilight song of the Wood-Pewee: A preliminary statement. *Auk* 43:150–52.

Red-eyed Vireo
- Allen quote from: Allen, Arthur A., and Peter P. Kellogg. 1954. *Songbirds of America in Color, Sound, and Story* (LP and book album). Houghton Mifflin Company and The Federation of Ontario Naturalists.
- Lawrence, L. K. 1954. The voluble singer of the tree-tops. *Audubon* 56:109–111.

Common Raven
- The Inuit creation myth can be found at http://ccrma.stanford.edu/~mburtner/winterraven.html.

Carolina Wren
- Morton, E. S. 1987. The effects of distance and isolation on song-type sharing in the Carolina Wren. *Wilson Bulletin* 99:601–10.

Winter Wren
- Brand quote from: Brand, Albert R. 1934. *Songs of Wild Birds*. New York: Thomas Nelson and Sons. Page 67.
- Burroughs quote from: Burroughs, John. 1895. *Wake-Robin*. Boston and New York: Houghton, Mifflin and Company. Page 43.
- Thoreau quote from his Journal entry of July 10, 1858. 1906. *The Writings of Henry David Thoreau,* vol. 9. Edited by Bradford Torrey. Boston and New York: Houghton, Mifflin and Company. Page 34.
- Kroodsma, D. E. 1980. Winter Wren singing behavior: A pinnacle of song complexity. *Condor* 82:357–365.

Eastern Bluebird
- Thoreau quote from his Journal entry of February 18, 1857. In Thoreau, *Writings,* vol. 9. Page 270.

American Robin
- For discussion of hawk-alarm calls among birds, see Marler, Peter, and Hans Slabbekoorn (editors). 2004. *Nature's Music.* San Diego: Elsevier Academic Press.

Wood Thrush
- Bent quote from: Bent, A. C. 1964. Life histories of North American thrushes, kinglets, and their allies. *U.S. National Museum Bulletin* 196:101.
- Thoreau quote from his Journal entry of July 5, 1852. In Thoreau, *Writings*, vol. 4. Page 191.

Thrush Flight Calls
- For more information about flight calls and to order *Flight Calls of Migratory Birds,* go to: www.oldbird.org.
- Evans, W. R. 2005. Monitoring avian night flight calls: The new century ahead. *Passenger Pigeon* 67:15–24.

Northern Mockingbird
- Burroughs quote from: Burroughs, John. 1895. *Birds and Poets with Other Papers.* Boston and New York: Houghton, Mifflin and Company. Page 8.

Ovenbird
- Excerpt from "The Oven Bird" in Frost, Robert. 1969. *The Poetry of Robert Frost.* Edited by Edward Connery Lathem. New York: 1969. Henry Holt and Company.
- Burroughs quote from: Burroughs, *Wake-Robin,* vol. 2. Page 53.
- Thoreau quote from his Journal entry dated June 11, 1851. In Thoreau, *Writings,* vol. 2.

Summer Tanager
- Researcher who verified my recording of Summer Tanager dawn song: W. Douglas Robinson, Department of Fisheries and Wildlife, Oregon State University, Corvallis, Oregon.

Scarlet Tanager
- Peterson quote from: Peterson, Roger Tory. 1980. *A Field Guide to the Birds of Eastern and Central North America,* 4th ed. Boston: Houghton Mifflin Company. Page 260.

Henslow's Sparrow
- Peterson quote from: Peterson, Roger Tory. 1947. *A Field Guide to the Birds,* 3rd ed. Boston: Houghton Mifflin Company. Page 231.

White-crowned Sparrow
- Baptista, L. F. 1975. Song dialects and demes in sedentary populations of the White-crowned Sparrow *(Zonotrichia leophrys nuttalli)* in the Sierra Nevada. *Condor* 77:145–53.

Bobolink
- Bent, A. C. 1958. Life histories of North American blackbirds, orioles, tanagers, and allies. *U.S. National Museum Bulletin* 211:44.
- Bryant poem from: Bryant, William C. 1883. *The Poetical Works of William Cullen Bryant,* vol. 2. Edited by Parke Godwin. New York: D. Appleton and Company. Page 41.
- Quote by Mathews from: Mathews, F. Schuyler. 1904. *Field Book of Wild Birds and Their Music.* New York: G. P. Putnam's Sons. Page 49.

Brown-headed Cowbird
- Elliott, Lang. 1999. *Music of the Birds.* Boston: Houghton Mifflin Company.

Baltimore Oriole
- Catesby, Mark. 1731. *The Natural History of Carolina, Florida, and the Bahama Islands,* vol. 1. London (self-published).
- Beletsky, L. D. 1982. Vocal behavior of the Northern Oriole. *Wilson Bulletin* 94: 372–80.

American Goldfinch
- Burroughs quote from: Burroughs, John. 1894. *Riverby.* Boston and New York: Houghton, Mifflin and Company. Page 84.

House Finch
- Information about courtship singing of the House Finch was obtained from personal communication with Dr. Geoffrey Hill, Department of Biological Sciences, Auburn University, Auburn, Alabama.

Photo Credits

The beautiful photographs that grace the pages of this book are the work of fifteen talented and dedicated nature photographers, including the author. Bird photography has blossomed in the last decade, coincident with the appearance of professional digital cameras. In this book, roughly half the images are derived from digital sources. The other half are from 35mm slides taken with traditional film cameras. Irrespective of source, the results are exceptional.

In the following list, images are identified by the page numbers on which they occur. Small inset photos are designated by an "i" after the page number. For pages 79 and 126, the photos are identified as A through D, listed clockwise beginning in the upper left for page 79 or lower left for page 126.

Doug Backlund — 49i
John Cancalosi — 19, 107i
John P. Duggan — 25
Lang Elliott — front cover, 1, 2, 3, 5, 6, 9, 10, 13, 14, 27, 27i, 39, 59i,
        69i, 77i, 79D, 81, 89, 101, 103, 105, 105i, 107, 117, 119, 120, 121, 126A
Wil Hershberger — 41, 43, 49, 51, 79B, 97
Nick Kontonicolas — 21
Maslowski Productions — 45, 65i, 79A, 79C, 83, 115
Garth McElroy — 33, 67, 87
Arthur Morris — 23, 31, 73
Marie Read — 29, 37, 39i, 53, 57, 61, 71, 83i, 85, 91, 93, 95, 111i, 113, 126B
Robert Royse — 47, 55, 65, 69, 99, 126C, 126D, 127
Brian E. Small — 17, 35, 45i, 59, 63, 75, 77, 109, 111
Julie Zickefoose — 51i
Daniella Theoret — 23i

Red-winged Blackbird   American Goldfinch   Scarlet Tanager   Grasshopper Sparrow

The Sound Recordings

All the field recordings featured on the compact disc were made by the author except for those listed below.

Borror Laboratory of Bioacoustics, Ohio State University (blb.biosci.ohio-state.edu):
    Donald Borror—Blue-gray Gnatcatcher (song)
Kevin Colver—Winter Wren (western song)
Bill Evans—American Bittern (flight calls), Barred Owl (pair calling), various thrushes (flight notes)
Dan Gibson—Eastern Screech-Owl (two pairs giving monotonic trills)
Wil Hershberger—Eastern Screech-Owl (whinny), Blue Jay (various calls)
Donald Kroodsma—Eastern Wood-Pewee (dawn song)
Macaulay Library, Cornell University Laboratory of Ornithology (www.animalbehaviorarchives.org):
    Gregory F. Budney—Northern Cardinal (female song)
    Arthur A. Allen—Ivory-billed Woodpecker (calls)
Ted Mack—Common Loon (yodels and tremolos), Sandhill Crane (unison calling), American Woodcock (flight display), Ovenbird (flight song), Western Meadowlark (flight song)
Eugene S. Morton—Carolina Wren duetting

Red-eyed Vireo

Index

*Page numbers in **bold** refer to photographs.*